Chasing Lions

by Amanda Marks

Antler House
Press

To George, Charlie and Mike,
Thanks for taking a chance on the girl
who once came third in a national
German poetry speaking competition.

Contents

PROLOGUE

I was sitting in the dark somewhere out the back of beyond by a river in the middle of Africa.

I was about to get myself fired from the best job I'd ever had and was ever likely to have.

It was 19th May 1991, I was twenty-seven and I was the leader of a six-month-long overland expedition across Africa from the UK to Zimbabwe. With me were my co-driver, Rob, and fourteen adventure-hungry travellers.

It had all been going so well but then one person's thoughtless ice cream in Algeria became the whole group's diarrhoeal downfall. By the time we reached Kano in northern Nigeria, we all ended up in hospital. The trauma of being so ill affected us all and relationships built up over the last two months started to unravel. Selfishness kicked in, nerves and tempers frayed, and bitchiness curdled all previous camaraderie. We were on a journey of a lifetime but right now it was no fun at all.

In a few days' time, we were going to hit the most difficult section of the trip, Zaire (now the Democratic Republic of Congo). Travelling through Africa's remote 'heart of darkness', we would be crossing endless swathes of emerald green rainforest. The red earth roads that forced their way through this immense wildwood served up a very good line in truck-eating mud holes and precarious log bridges guaranteed to bring out any driver in a cold sweat. If we couldn't work together or help and trust each other, we'd struggle to get safely through the rigours of a month in the tropical forests of this vast country.

Someone had to rally the group. As leader, that someone should have been me but I'd been trying without success for the three weeks since we left hospital. I could only think of one last strategy: to tell them the harsh truth about their behaviour, no punches pulled. Either I would shock them into once again becoming the decent human beings I knew them to be — a long shot, I had to admit — or I'd be on the next flight out of Bangui and a new leader would have to be sent to replace me. I didn't like the odds. Bugger.

Two years previously, I'd hit the road hoping to see lions in the wild and discover the courage I thought I lacked. This is the story of some of the adventures of my 55,000-mile journey through the Middle East and Africa in a sixteen-ton truck. It was a journey that ultimately helped me find not only lions but my place in the world.

PART ONE

THE JOURNEY BEGINS

CHAPTER ONE

A silent mugging

When I was twenty-two, I was mugged. It was one of the best things that ever happened to me.

I was mugged again when I was twenty-six. Most people would consider this to be rather bad luck.

The third time someone tried to mug me, I was having none of it.

I'm quite a small person; five foot two and a quarter if I stand up very straight. When they attacked, my instinct was to make myself even smaller. I shrank. There on the frozen ground of the park, with snow flurries whipping around me in the darkness, I curled up into a tight ball and prayed that the many pairs of boots around me wouldn't make contact. Groping hands quickly relieved me of my backpack, then I was left; a spineless hedgehog in pink woolly gloves.

I hadn't fought. I hadn't screamed. I hadn't uttered a sound. It was a silent mugging. Even the muggers were voiceless — or, at least, that's the way I remember it.

That was my first mugging.

It was March 1986 and I was a final-year French and German student at Leeds University. I should probably tell you that my attackers were a bunch of knife-wielding thugs and I was lucky to get away with my life. That would certainly be far more dramatic than the truth which is that I was done over by a group of delinquent twelve-year-olds. They got away with a rather mediocre essay on the formalities of the French language in business — I wished them joy of it; my purse — they wouldn't find much in there; and my Sony Walkman — now that was upsetting. The thing that really annoyed me, though, was that I didn't even scream. For God's sake! Surely you're supposed to scream if you're being mugged? It was pathetic or, more precisely, I was pathetic.

The incident took me right back to being a seven-year-old, and the time my best friend hit me and then pushed me out of her front yard with a broom. I was like a toy she'd finished playing with and she was now sweeping me away, out of sight, unwanted. I didn't understand what I'd done, I didn't ask, I didn't tell her to stop, I didn't hit back, I just ran home in tears, mortified with hurt. My dad's easy reaction was to say, 'Well, just go and hit her back.' But I couldn't. She was my friend, my best friend. I must have done something wrong or surely she wouldn't have done that to me. All I could do was shrink, and wait and hope for her to be nice to me again. Was that where it started, this feeling of never *quite* measuring up or belonging, never *quite* being good enough, and always wondering whether I might say something or do something to make people dislike me? Could such an insignificant thing as a temporary falling out between seven-year-old friends affect a person's confidence for a lifetime? Maybe.

I'd kept my lack of confidence quite well hidden under a layer of competence and through having a decent dose of good northern pragmatism thanks to my Yorkshire parents. I was certainly on the shy side and I was never someone who enjoyed parties, but I had a small group of close friends. I was probably never going to do anything dramatic or exciting in my life, and I didn't have huge ambitions other than to have a good life filled with love, family, cats and dogs, and maybe a horse. But I was happy in my little world.

Those sixty seconds of panic in the dark in a freezing cold park in Yorkshire changed things. I felt like a victim and I didn't like it. Things had to change. I had to change. I needed to be stronger, braver, to stop being such a bystander and, instead, take part and make decisions about what I wanted rather than just letting things happen. I'd read enough stories to dream of being an adventurous and courageous character. *The Lion, The Witch and The Wardrobe* was still one of my favourite books and I envied Lucy fighting alongside Aslan. When I took up fencing later that week I knew that wasn't really the answer but I was determined to start channelling more lion and less mouse.

'Do you fancy coming to this slideshow talk tonight?' asked Sheena, my good friend and housemate, as we drove home from the office.

Sheena and I met when we joined a marketing agency in Gloucestershire in late summer 1986 and now, just over a year later, we were both account managers looking after insurance companies and large agrochemical businesses. By most people's reckoning, we were on a good career path and doing very well for ourselves. We'd bought a tiny, terraced house in Swindon together, so we had a mortgage and were feeling very grown-up.

I thought a life in the advertising world would be exciting and a real challenge. I felt I'd gone out and grabbed life by the horns. But, after about a year, I noticed my desk turning into a millstone and the sparkle wearing off the business meetings in London and lunches in posh restaurants. It began to dawn on me that I didn't care too much about adding to the success of these large corporate clients. So, at the same time as trying to live the life of a successful eighties' businesswoman, complete with obligatory shoulder pads, I found myself needing to constantly escape. Sheena felt the same, so whenever we could, we went off hiking and travelling in the UK and Europe.

What was I doing about the urge to do something different? Nothing. I hadn't a clue what I wanted other than to be a vet, which I wasn't clever enough for. And, if I'm honest, I was too scared to go out on a limb to try and find something else and risk losing all I now had. This was my world. I had a good job, prospects, friends, a house and a reasonable salary. I wasn't unhappy. That was good enough, wasn't it? So I carried on, and told myself that this was right for me, that I was lucky to have this.

The talk that Sheena invited me to was at the Royal Agricultural College. The evening was a revelation.

The speaker, Charlie Hopkinson, was no farmer. He was a director of an overland adventure company. For well over an hour, he regaled a rapt audience with stories about journeys across the length of Africa or along the Hippy Trail to Kathmandu. We saw images of iconic sites such as the Taj Mahal. We oohed at elephants and lions in the Serengeti. We smiled at sun-tanned people in scruffy clothes standing by Victoria Falls or shopping for food in local markets. We wowed at the truck which carried the travellers and the tents they slept in. We heard of dramas and difficulties, laughs and friendships. We heard of a different life. I was entranced.

I took a brochure home and pored over every inch of it — all the itineraries, all the photos, and all the maps. I love maps. Page after page of thrilling adventures beckoned me. Could I be part of such an exciting life for a short time? Why not? I could go to Africa and see lions in the wild, something I'd always wanted to do. I could hear them calling to me already.

The shortest and cheapest Africa trip was three weeks long but I really wanted to do the five weeks from Nairobi to Harare. Could I cope with camping in a tent? I'd only ever been in a camper van. What if I didn't like the other people? They were bound to be far more adventurous than me, probably not the kind of people I was used to, but surely it would be fun for a few weeks. According to Charlie, quite a few passengers would be Australian. Would I like Australians? Why wouldn't I? And how could I manage to cook for twenty people . . . on a fire! Would it even be safe? What if something awful happened in the middle of nowhere? What if I got malaria?

My list of questions grew by the day so, in the end, Sheena suggested I ring the company, Dragoman.

'You'll just end up talking yourself out of it if you don't call them. Just ring, for heaven's sake.' She laughed at my dithering. 'You've got to. You'll kick yourself if you don't, and I don't think you having a few weeks off will bring ICI or the Prudential to their knees. It's just a holiday. It's not like you're planning to circumnavigate the globe.'

'Yes but . . .'

Sheena picked up the phone and the brochure, dialled the number, then handed the receiver to me and sat down, watching me.

'Oh, hi. Er, I . . . Can I talk to Charlie please?

Sheena gave me the thumbs up and grinned.

'Charlie, hi. I came to your talk a couple of weeks ago in Cirencester. Yes, I really enjoyed it, thanks. I was just . . . well, I had some questions, if you don't mind. Great. So . . . so how do I become a tour leader in Africa?'

I saw Sheena's jaw drop and, as I listened to Charlie, I put my hand over my mouth to stop the escape of any telltale squeaks of excitement or astonishment. Never mind Sheena, I'd just shocked myself.

When I put the phone down about ten minutes later, Sheena and I both screamed and laughed hysterically.

'What have you done?!' she said.

'I don't know, but it feels good!'

CHAPTER TWO

It'll fuck up your life

It did indeed feel good but it was also extremely daunting.

Charlie hadn't exactly brimmed with enthusiasm when I asked about joining the company as a tour leader. I guess he'd have preferred to sell a holiday. But he did put me in touch with one of his two partners, George, who was in charge of the trucks and the leaders. Speaking to George the following day, the reality hit as to what I might be letting myself in for.

'You'll need a heavy goods vehicle licence, at least HGV 2, and, of course, you need reasonable competence at diesel mechanics. Do you have either of those?'

'No, I'm afraid not.'

'Any skill in *anything* practical?'

'Er, I decorated my house. Does that count?' This wasn't sounding great.

'Okay, no worries. Well, why don't you call me when you've got an HGV licence and learned some mechanics, and we can see about things then. Okay?'

He wasn't exactly unfriendly but he sounded somewhere between bored and depressed. I couldn't quite work him out. Was I expected to take his lack of enthusiasm as a brush-off? It would have been very easy to give it up as a bad idea and just pay to be a passenger instead, but he hadn't actually said 'no'. A streak of stubbornness kicked in. I was damned if I wouldn't give it a go. If I failed at learning mechanics or didn't pass the truck driving test, well, that would be my answer — it obviously wasn't meant to be.

Over the next few months, I took evening classes in car mechanics and my bedtime reading was a Haynes manual. When I say it didn't come easily . . . Oh, who was I kidding? I'd never be able to do this. I was good at foreign languages but the language of mechanics was from a different planet. It was like being back at school, with a physics teacher flattening my hopes of becoming a vet in one fell swoop: 'Physics and Chemistry A Level? No, I don't think so, do you, Amanda?'

Diesel mechanics? Do we really think so, Amanda?

After three months, I was very close to giving up. Then my HGV lessons started. There was the initial hiccup of not being able to quite reach the pedals, but my instructor — a burly ex-truck-driver in his fifties — took it in his stride, found cushions to put behind my back, and off we went. I was the first woman he'd taught to drive a truck and I got the distinct impression that he was taking me on as a laugh. As it happened, though, me and truck-driving hit it off straight away. I loved it! I loved the height of the cab, the feeling of being in charge of such a large machine, going to truck stops for greasy bacon sandwiches and the banter with the other drivers who firstly stared but then encouraged me . . . I loved that I could do it.

The unexpected success with the HGV lessons pushed me to renewed efforts with learning mechanics and slowly but surely some of it began to sink in. Confident, I wasn't, but I was hopeful that I might be able to learn enough to get my foot in the door at Dragoman. In late November, I passed my HGV test. I was a truck driver!

Full of puppy dog enthusiasm, I rang George.

'Oh right, well done. You'd best come over and see us then. Come in January and stay for the night. Bring some dirty clothes.'

I couldn't hear a smile behind his words. He was probably surprised — maybe even disappointed — to hear from me. But was I still chuffed to bits to be going for an interview? You could say!

Dragoman was based in rural Suffolk on a farm called Camp Green. Getting there was a feat in itself. It was too far for my unreliable car, so I took the train to London, then to Ipswich, then a bus to the nearest small village, then walked about a mile to reach the farm. In the yard, as well as the usual farming paraphernalia, there was the skeleton of an old truck plus huge tyres and chunks of metal. A couple of young guys in dirty jeans and sweatshirts were hammering at the metal, and a man in grubby grey overalls was standing with a mug in hand watching them. He was in his mid-thirties and had a full moon face. He seemed deep in thought. He looked up and saw me.

'Oh, hello. I'm George,' he said, in that flat, almost depressed tone I vaguely remembered from our phone conversations. 'I suppose you're Amanda.' We shook hands, and the other two men stopped working to say hi.

'So you passed your HGV. Good. How are the mechanics coming along? No worries, I'll show you round first.'

Thank God he didn't wait for an answer about the mechanics.

I met so many people and was introduced to so many new words, nicknames and turns of phrase that morning that it all became a bit of a blur. There was a small office where the 'shiny bums' worked. Some of the trainees slept in a wreck of a caravan they called the Dog Box or 'Old Dogger'. An old black Mercedes van was known as 'Van de Merc', and firewood was called *kuni*, which was Swahili, apparently.

Lunch in the brick-built 'New Dogger' with George and the current crew at the farm was a funny affair. We ate soup and cheese on toast while everyone made fun of each other good-humouredly and laughed about stories from their travels or things going on at the farm.

After lunch, I was given a riveter. Me. A riveter! This thing looked dangerous. It had a handle on one end, a thick nozzle on the other, and in between was a metal concertina contraption. The idea was that you extended the concertina, pushed a metal rivet in the nozzle, placed said rivet in a prepared hole in some metal sheeting, then tried to close the concertina. I nearly gave myself a black eye, I broke a few rivets, and I smashed my hand more than once. When I actually managed to put in a line of rivets I was stupidly pleased with myself. Then I was handed a grease gun.

'Do you think you can cope with greasing the prop shaft? You'll see the nipples. Shout if you're not sure.'

Trucks have nipples? I wasn't sure that had been in my mechanics lessons.

The greasing didn't last very long in the end, though, as George came into the workshop and asked everyone to jump in the back of the van.

'We've got to go and round up some sheep,' he explained. Was this yet another peculiar turn of phrase for some unknown mechanics task? No. Sure enough, after a short drive, me and four others piled out of the back of Van de Merc and went chasing around an orchard hot on the heels of a small flock of escaped sheep. That was a first! This was certainly an interview like no other.

Thankfully, I didn't have to sleep in the Dogger that night.

Instead, I was the guest of Di and Douglas — known as the *memsahib* and the *bwana* — George's charming parents and owners of the farm. They used to farm in Kenya so that explained why Swahili words kept cropping up.

By the time I went to bed that night, I was both shattered and buzzing. This wasn't like anything I'd come across before. There was no doubt that I was a fish out of water, but this fish was looking for a new river and very much liked the flow of this one.

The next morning, George came to say goodbye before I headed off for my bus. Had I passed the 'interview'?

'What do you think then?' he asked.

'I think I'd love to be part of this, but I know I've got a lot to learn.'

He smiled.

'You know, it'll fuck up your life.'

His voice was deadpan but there was a glint in his eyes.

CHAPTER THREE
Grease monkey

I arrived at Camp Green feeling like an imposter who'd got in by accident and would be found out at any moment. I was keenly aware that this could turn out to be the most short-lived and embarrassing interlude of my life.

It was August 1988, I was twenty-four and I was embarking on a totally new and completely alien way of life. The house was sold, I'd got rid of my car, stored personal belongings with my folks, swapped the business skirts and blouses for comfortable, scruffy clothes, bought a sleeping bag and some walking boots, and headed to Dragoman's base in Suffolk. No more reasonably well-paid job and comfortable lifestyle for me. My new home for the next few months was in a grubby workshop on a farm just behind the back of beyond, where I had an uncomfortable bunk in a knackered old caravan. Based here, I was to earn £2.50 a day (out of which I had to eat) for working seven days a week helping to turn a sixteen-ton Mercedes supermarket lorry into an overland truck that would carry up to twenty-three passengers on a journey of a lifetime. The truck and I were on the same trajectory, undergoing a major overhaul to become fit for an adventure. I just hoped the process wouldn't break me before I got the prize at the end of the road: a journey through Africa.

I've never been work-shy but at that time neither had I ever actually done much hard physical work. I wasn't unfit but, let's face it, a bit of sport, some house decorating, horse riding and mucking out the occasional stable didn't exactly add up to hard graft. In my ever-expanding Dragoman terminology, I was a shiny-bum and I was trying to transform myself into a grease monkey.

It wasn't the hard work per se that bothered me but I was keenly aware that my mechanical knowledge and practical know-how were superficial at best. What made it worse was that all the other trainees and crew at the farm seemed to be supremely confident and practical beings who were either the offspring of farmers, builders, truck drivers or engineering graduates. How on earth would I — the girl who once came third in a national German poetry-speaking competition — measure up? What was I thinking trying to do this?

The answer was simple in some ways: I just *really* wanted to. I wanted to find the courage to have an adventure that meant something to me, that stretched me, and that showed me the world and my place within it. I wanted to understand too — exactly *what* I wanted to understand I'm not sure but I sometimes felt that everyone around me knew the rules of the game and I didn't even know the name.

'Cup!' shouted Mr Clean, as he put an empty mug on the floor in the room next to me.

Morning in the Old Dogger had begun. Stevie 'Clean' had long since given up putting tea in said cup as it always ended up stone cold by the time Lutey surfaced. But, having made his roommate vaguely aware that it was morning, he brought in a proper cup of tea to my tiny room — a bit of indulgence to start my day. Bless him. Stevie was always up with the sparrows and the man was a wonder of cheerfulness, organisation and cleanliness. He had his standards and overlanding wasn't going to compromise them. He even ironed his clothes, a unique foible in this world of muck and make-do.

Every night in bed my arms would get spasms of pins and needles. Perhaps it was their way of telling me to stop all this nonsense? But by morning I was ready to go again, and by eight o'clock, Stevie and I hit the workshop along with the rest of the crew who were living around the farm. Lutey would usually only manage to stagger out by about nine o'clock. Once he was up, though, it was as if someone had flicked a switch at the back of his head. Off he went. He was a Cornish powerhouse of mad enthusiasm and genuine friendliness. My fellow Old Dogger trainees were just two of the diverse characters I came to know and love as we shared the hard graft we hoped would get us a place as a trainee co-driver, and eventually as a leader, on one of the epic road journeys we were here to experience.

I was only the fourth woman Dragoman had taken on since they began in 1981. Around the time I joined there was a small influx of female trainee drivers. We were some of the first women commercial overland drivers in the world. I'm quite glad that didn't dawn on me at the time.

Commercial overlanding had been around since the 1960s, mostly offering the famous 'Hippy Trail' to India and Kathmandu until 1979 when Russia invaded Afghanistan and the Islamic Revolution made Iran out of bounds. In those early days, the role of overland driver was most definitely a bastion of masculinity, and even when the number of companies and trips grew in the early 1980s, the position was still very male-dominated. Some companies outright refused to employ women, others graciously allowed them to be couriers, which were like a host or organiser, but not leader-drivers. Dragoman seemed to be almost unique in realising that having some female driving crew was a positive.

All the Dragowomen knew we had to prove we could do what was needed. In a truck-building workshop, heavy lifting was needed much of the time. For all of us, this was an every day, whole body workout. If the only way we could shift something was to sit on the floor and use our legs to push, so be it. We added extra length onto spanners to get more leverage for undoing super tight bolts, and we learned to use two long tyre levers to help us lift the ridiculously heavy wheels onto the hubs. There was always a way. After just a few days, the well-dressed advertising executive was gone. It was impossible to get my hands properly clean and I'd taken numerous chunks out of them. I was bruised all over and hurt in places I never normally considered — I'm sure even my hair hurt some days. Certainly, I learned and got better, but soon everyone knew that if something was going to go wrong there was a fair bet it was going to happen to me.

'Amanda, can you get rid of this please?' asked George, or G as he was known. It was a tank full of waste oil which I had to pour into the main waste oil tank. Tripping over my own feet, it was a classic will-she-won't-she moment. I tried to right myself but, of course, no, down I went. Dirty oil launched itself like a rogue wave to splatter a huge area of the workshop floor. What can you say? 'Sorry' didn't seem quite enough. I wanted the ground to open up beneath me. Instead, I did the only thing I could — I started cleaning up. Thankfully Lutey and others quickly came to help. G's face was a picture of expressionless eloquence.

Drill bits were my nemesis. It didn't matter what I was putting a hole into, I broke them as if they were matchsticks. As for welding . . . But then there was the day I successfully attached a windscreen wiper system — motor and all. I even got it working. Success! There was just one small thing wrong so I took the wiper off again and . . . promptly snapped it in half. G must have rued the day he took me on.

On the plus side, though, I quickly got the hang of the initially dreaded concertina riveter, and the angle-grinder no longer held any fears for me when cutting bits of steel. I even quite liked the sharp smell of burning hot metal and the high-pitched whine like a mosquito on steroids. I was confidently greasing anything that moved from steering columns to ball joints and spring king pins. Soon, I could change a truck tyre safely, replace brake shoes and even put in a new clutch (with help). It was a surprise to learn that truck springs were bloody great slabs of tapered steel lying one on top of another instead of the coils of metal I'd expected, but even changing these heavy beasts soon became second nature. I also did a whole heap of donkey work backing the more able mechanics and body builders in the Drago team: masking the windows and other parts of the truck prior to it being spray-painted; painting wheel hubs, steel box section and even tables and chairs; cleaning and mending fridges; ensuring the efficient sliding of the windows through copious additions of silicone spray; and checking, sorting and labelling the heavy A-frame tents — lots of them.

'Do you think I might be able to get my first trip soon, G?' I asked after about six months had gone by. Some trainees were in and out within a few months but nothing had been mentioned to me.

'Hmm, you're doing well and you've learned a lot, but . . .

well, it does seem like you have a total lack of spatial awareness.' He said it in his usual understated, matter-of-fact way, and I wasn't surprised, but it still hurt.

Spatial awareness was one of G's *things*. If you didn't have it you would make mistakes. In my case, it seemed to be like a missing gene. I could see that I was often a huge frustration to him — a frustration I completely understood as I felt it acutely myself. My path to adequate mechanical and practical competence was a rather steep and tortuous one. I rose, I fell, I climbed a little higher, I stumbled back down. But I didn't give in and I felt sure I was heading in the right direction. Someone with less patience and generosity of spirit would have had me out of the door within weeks of my arrival, but not G, even though there were times I'm certain he'd have liked to. Perhaps he stuck with me because he could see I tried so hard and he believed in people who put in the effort. G was someone all the Dragoman crew loved, laughed with, learned from and worked hard for.

Later that month, I was testing some electrics I'd just wired in. I pressed what I thought was the right button and immediately the most god-awful clattering and banging came from the engine. My heart stopped. My breathing stopped. I had an almost out-of-body experience seeing myself sitting in the driver's seat of the truck, unable to move, think or react. Slowly, I looked down at what I'd pressed. It was the engine starter button. Christ! The engine wasn't quite completed. I'd done it now. This was no small accident to be laughed off or apologised for. This was huge. Hours of painstaking work and expense had gone into getting the engine to the pristine state it was in — clean smooth steel internal workings fine-tuned with precision. I had just fucked up the whole thing. This was bound to be a sackable offence. I understood enough to know that the whole engine would have to be stripped down as connecting rods and pistons would be mangled. Everyone had stopped what they were doing and were looking at either me or G.

'Why don't you go home, Amanda?' suggested G, through tightly gritted teeth.

I don't know if he meant me to just have a few hours in the Dogger, but I packed a small backpack and left the farm. I'd just ruined everything. That was it. There was no way they'd let me out on the road now. I took a train north, back to my folks' home in Durham. The self-confidence I'd been nurturing for seven long months had just vanished into thin air. I was gutted.

It took me three days of Mum's care and home-cooked food and Dad's relentless positivity and encouragement, a comfy bed, three long snowy walks over the fells with the dog, and a couple of much-needed hot bubble baths before I found the courage to call G.

'Oh, hi Amanda,' he said, in his usual Eeyore tones.

'I'm so sorry about the engine, G. I can't believe I did that.'

'No worries, we fixed it. Are you coming back soon? Everyone's jelly-bagging about getting the truck finished so it would be good to get the help.'

How I didn't yell with delight down the phone I have no idea. He hadn't sacked me. I could go back. I doubt anyone has ever been so pleased to abandon home comforts for a freezing cold caravan that let in the snow.

I was back at the farm two days later and it took us another two weeks to see this latest truck off on its travels. It felt like an achievement — it *was* an achievement — and we all celebrated with a Dogger party after saying goodbye to the crew and passengers at Harwich. They were headed to India. I wondered when it might be me in their place.

'I'm sorry we couldn't put you on that trip, Amanda,' said G, later that night. 'We needed someone with an Aussie or Kiwi passport, I'm afraid. But I've pencilled you in for the trip with Freddie in July. That's the next one to go. It's an eight-week Middle East and Egypt circuit.'

Oh my God! Okay, so it's not Africa, well, Egypt is, obviously, but ... Oh my God, I'm going on a trip!

I'd never even heard of Freddie but apparently he would be arriving back in the workshop about three weeks before our trip (*our* trip!) and, of course, we had to get our truck (*our* truck!) ready in that time. Yes, that meant a few more weeks of hard work to come, but that was fine. I was going to be a trainee co-driver on an overland journey through Egypt, Jordan, Syria and Turkey via Europe at the start and end. I was a happy little grease monkey.

PART TWO

EGYPT & THE MIDDLE EAST

CHAPTER FOUR
The serf

'Watch out, he's going!'

Freddie was an energetic, dark-haired, strongly built young chap who looked as if he wouldn't think twice about enjoying a heavy night after a long day's work. In reality, he regularly tended to fall asleep early on in the evening. The group got used to seeing an inane grin spread over his face then his eyes start to swim before his forehead ended up in his dinner. It was very funny and rather endearing. He was Dennis the Menace on the outside and Pooh Bear on the inside.

My trainee trip with him was as exciting and fascinating as it was initially daunting and continuously challenging. Freddie was a lovely bloke with a good sense of humour and he was very willing to share all the knowledge he'd gleaned from his previous trips. He got frustrated with my driving at times as he felt I drove too slowly, but we still shared the driving equally. He was extremely competent with the mechanics and I took on more of the planning as well as continually learning more under his supervision and doing general truck maintenance. Freddie loved pleasing people, especially the girls. He was an outrageous but good-natured flirt. He cajoled everyone into enjoying themselves and was always up for a giggle. Being a morning person, he was usually up before most others and took delight in putting on music loudly once he thought everyone should be out of bed. His track of choice was usually *'Good Morning, Vietnam'* by Robin Williams from the movie of the same name. At the end of eight weeks, we knew the words to all the songs on that cassette by heart. To this day, it remains the soundtrack of that trip for me.

After that first tour, I was ridiculously happy to be given the role of leader on the next circuit. I'd done it. I was an overland tour leader. Against all the odds, I'd actually succeeded!

Sadly, it was my bad luck to be matched with a trainee co-driver called Ryan. Ryan didn't see why he should be the sidekick to a 'young girlie' and took great delight in undermining me whenever he could. Just what I needed on my first trip as a leader. Thank goodness for a wonderful set of passengers, otherwise I think my overlanding career might have come to a rather premature end.

And now, I was on my third Egypt and Middle East trip — my second as a tour leader. The night ferry taking us across to Belgium was swaying horribly and I was trying hard not to throw up. I lay in my bed watching the still form on the narrow bunk opposite me. It was Guy's first trip with Dragoman.

Please don't let him be another Ryan, I prayed silently. I really didn't think I deserved another chauvinistic sod. I'd been looking forward to leading and sharing all the knowledge I had about the places we were travelling through — places I'd come to love. There was no sharing anything other than driving and work with Ryan, and he wasn't even too keen on that since anything I asked him to do seemed to demean his manhood.

My first impressions of Guy when I arrived back in the workshop after my trip with Ryan were not what you might call favourable. Although I didn't dislike him, two weeks on I still figured him to be a cocky, self-opinionated southerner who smoked and drank far too much and was difficult to hold a conversation with. Not that I was being at all judgemental! On the plus side though, he was very easy on the eye, tall and slim with waves of almost black hair, he could play the guitar well, and he was happy to entertain people with his songs which was something I admired. Perhaps there was *some* hope.

We were responsible for a group of fifteen passengers from the UK, Australia and New Zealand. I now knew to expect that they would look to us, me in particular, to be the fount of all knowledge for the next eight weeks.

'How high are the pyramids, Amanda?' Fair enough.

'Can I buy tomatoes in the next village?' Well, if they're selling them.

'What time does the bank open on a Thursday in Asyut?' Funny, I didn't feel the need to know that on my last visit.

'If I ring my mother will she be in?' I mean, what can you say?

Overland passengers are mostly an interesting, broad-minded, fun-loving bunch of people who are a pleasure to travel with and who have a genuine curiosity about the people and places they've come to see. But there did seem to be a tendency for a very small proportion of them to leave all vestiges of good sense at home and others who developed outlandish expectations of their tour leaders. Male tour leaders, in particular, often found that they were endowed with an almost heroic stature in the eyes of certain passengers, and their sexual prowess, however mythical, was legendary. Did any take advantage of such a dreadful situation? How could you think such a thing?

It was certainly true that being a tour leader demanded a lot of you. In which other job would you be chief truck driver and bush mechanic, navigator extraordinaire, substitute nurse and part-time psychologist, accountant, translator, guide, and guardian for up to twenty-three people? After taking all this in their stride day in and day out, it's not surprising that some leaders felt they could cope with anything life threw at them. And some could. Unfortunately, I was not yet in that happy situation. I still tended to wonder when the bubble would burst and I would be seen as the rather bungling character I often felt like. It still surprised me when people listened to me, never mind actually did what I suggested. True, I had developed a good knowledge of the areas I was about to travel through once more, but where was that feeling of worldliness I'd thought would come with the job?

A persistent knocking at the door woke me up. It was the 6.15 a.m wake-up call that everyone in the drivers' quarters of the Harwich to Holland ferry was treated to.

'Thanks,' I croaked, and staggered to the shower to wake myself up, prodding Guy on the way. I got a muffled groan in reply. I'm a fairly annoying morning person. Guy, I was soon to discover, needed about two hours, three cups of strong black coffee and at least two cigarettes before he was safe to talk to, irrespective of what hour he woke. Blissfully unaware of this at the time, I poked him again as I left for the canteen armed with my maps of Europe. By the time he joined me, clutching his hot black link between sleep and wakefulness, I'd polished off a huge English breakfast and was trying to decide which road to take to get to our first stop of St Goar on the Rhine in Germany. I knew the roads well once I reached Egypt but there was just too much choice on European roads.

'I think we'll stop at the Brugge campsite before we get going,' I began, 'and make breakfast for them all. Then we can stop at some services to make lunch and we should get to St Goar by about four o'clock. We'd better fill up with diesel while we're in Belgium, at least enough to get to Greece anyway. Do you know how much we've got in the tanks? I forgot to check and I noticed the gauge doesn't work.'

'I've no idea,' said Guy. 'Charlie took her to Bristol on a roadshow about three weeks ago though, so he must have left some in the tank or he'd have told us. Shall we go and find the group before they start worrying we've slept in?'

They'd all congregated in the bar again and it seemed that after only one night some of them were like old friends. It was a good sign. The first few days could make or break a trip. I found that just keeping myself busy and watching the dynamics of the group was the best plan at first. Even after just one evening, though, three people had begun to make an impression on me. There was an attractive girl named Kathy who seemed to be travelling with Dave, both Australian and in their mid-twenties. The other was a nineteen-year-old, very tanned English public schoolboy called Tom. He reminded me of an excited puppy and had been bursting to tell me last night that he knew all about overlanding because he'd just come from three weeks in India with another trip led by my friend and fellow Dragowoman, Yve. Yve had a big heart, a big personality and ran her trips not only with a determination to have fun but with a will of iron — you wouldn't dare *not* have a good time if you were on one of her trips. Tom was going to see a big difference in leadership style.

We were off the ferry and through customs in no time and started down the motorway towards Brugge campsite for breakfast. About five minutes down the road the truck spluttered. I ignored it, thinking it was just early morning blues, and carried on. Two minutes later, we slowly ground to a halt at the side of the road as we lost all power.

'I don't believe this is happening. Guy, tell me I'm dreaming and that we haven't just run out of fuel after ten minutes on the road.'

'Where do you go? Who do you see? Which way do you turn?' he said, with a smile and a shrug of the shoulders.

'Er . . . okay.' I didn't really know how to respond to that.

I breathed deeply before turning round to the mystified passengers and explaining that we'd just run out of fuel. I was far too embarrassed to wait for a reaction. I just got out of the truck, grabbed a couple of jerry cans and took the walk of shame with Guy to the nearest fuel station.

Well, that's it, I thought to myself as I stomped down the road half an hour later lugging a heavy jerry can back to the stranded truck. They're never going to trust me now. They'll think I'm stupid and incompetent. I am. Why the bloody hell didn't I check the fuel? And Guy will think he's going to be trained by a complete prat.

It was a memorable start to the trip, but definitely not in a way I'd have liked. By the time we reached the campsite in the afternoon, the group seemed happy enough, though. Guy and I helped everyone set up camp and find their way around the truck, and after my talk about safety and security, we shared out the many jobs that needed doing on the truck for the next eight weeks. We called them wallahships. Dave was to be kitty-wallah, looking after the group's pooled money that we used for food and camping. Kathy was a nurse so there was our first-aid wallah. Tom was desperate to be bar-wallah, an important job which had a lot of influence on group morale, and Will, a lovely, lanky Dutch guy became our water-wallah. Then there were back-locker packers, box-wallahs, people to clean the inside of the truck . . . there was a job for everyone. This was not silver-service camping, everyone had to muck in. People also formed themselves into teams of two or three people for cooking and washing up duties. They would soon get used to the plate-flapping dance known to all overlanders as the preferred drying method since tea towels all too quickly became pointlessly soggy objects.

As everyone pottered around getting their bags and tents sorted, Guy slaved over hot stoves with the help of Tom, who already knew the ropes.

'Grub's up!' shouted Guy, eventually. 'Anyone fancy chicken in peanut sauce with rice? Come and help yourselves.'

A rush of hungry people lined up by the large cook tables, loaded their red melamine plate with the divine-smelling dinner, and grabbed one of the canvas stools that had been arranged in a rough semi-circle.

It was quite late by the time we'd all helped clean up but everyone was still game to pile into the campsite bar for a few drinks. Later still came the first of many nights of campfire entertainment with Guy and an Australian called Pete on their guitars. Between them they had a huge repertoire, though only Guy could sing — actually he had a good singing voice. By the end of the trip, we would all have learned how to sing *Here comes the sun* in a Cockney accent, and we'd know all the words of Chris de Burgh's *Patricia the Stripper* and the chorus of *American Pie*.

By the time I went to bed that night, I'd convinced myself that the bad start was behind me and things could only get better from here on in.

A couple of days later, we were on a motorway heading for Yugoslavia. Fifteen minutes after leaving a service station, I heard a voice ask calmly, 'Where's Tom?'

'What?' I said, gripping the steering wheel tighter. 'Where's Tom? What do you mean? You can't have lost him back there!'

No Tom. Oh my God, first no fuel and now I was losing passengers. This was not good. Not good at all.

It took almost half an hour to get off the motorway, turn around and get back to the services. I was frantic in case Tom had decided to be clever and hitch to the border to meet us. There were two border posts nearby and he wouldn't know which one we were using.

Thankfully, luck was on my side. Tom had decided to have faith in me returning to find him and was lying outstretched soaking up the sun in the car park. He'd obviously found it hard to believe that we'd miss him for long, and it was an ideal chance for him to keep ahead of Guy on the 'I'm browner than you are' stakes. Guy, who sported pale olive skin at the start of the trip had bet berry-brown Tom that he would be darker than him in two weeks. Tom wasn't taking any chances and kept his arm permanently out of the windows when we were driving along, being sure to change sides each day.

'Where the hell did you go to?' Guy yelled at him in mock anger. 'Didn't your mother ever tell you not to wander off in strange service stations? Get in, we've got another ten thousand kilometres to go before we get home.'

Hmm, maybe I could get used to Guy. I liked the easy way he dealt with people and lightened moods. Definitely not like Ryan, thank goodness. Ryan would have made me feel more of a useless idiot than I already felt, but Guy managed to make a joke of it and

31

help me save face in front of the group, who were now laughing.

The rest of Europe passed fairly smoothly, and after a week we were at Piraeus in Greece where we boarded the overnight ferry to take us across the Mediterranean to Alexandria in Egypt.

Now, I'm not a big drinker. I never have been. I drink, but rarely overly much. Perhaps it was the relief of getting everyone here safely after the dismal start, or the fact that we had such a good group of people I felt comfortable with, or that I didn't have to fight my corner all the time with my co-driver as I had last time, or perhaps it was Kathy and Dave's impromptu cocktail bar and the singing and dancing with the Italian sailors. Whatever the reason, I totally let my guard down and got completely and utterly plastered on the ferry. It was one hell of a night, but, boy, did I pay for it.

On arrival at the port in Alexandria the next morning, I was frankly incapable. There was no way I could drive, I could barely sit up, so I had to just tell Guy to sort all the red tape at the port. It's no easy task when you've not done it before, as you have to go from one little shack to another filling in forms, showing passports, giving truck details, and getting men to come and check engine numbers and carnets. I was not proud but there was nothing I could do about it. At one point, Guy brought a man over to see me as he wanted to see the drivers.

'You are the driver?'

'Yes.'

'You drive this truck?' He obviously thought I hadn't understood him.

'Yes, I drive this truck. Guy is my co-driver.'

A broad smile began to widen across the man's initially serious face.

'And so he is your serf?'

Guy rolled his eyes but the official fell about laughing.

'Your serf is doing a good job. Marhaba. Welcome!' He slapped Guy on the back and they both went off to complete the documentation.

Later that morning, my hangover beginning to abate, we dropped the group at the market in Alexandria while Guy and I went to fill up with shockingly cheap diesel at 2p per litre. I was taken aback when the man at the petrol station welcomed me like a long-lost friend: 'Ah, Amanda! Welcome!' I guess they didn't get too many female truck drivers.

'Come on,' I said to Guy afterwards, 'I think I owe you lunch by way of an apology for this morning. Will a chicken sandwich and carcadet tea in a good hotel coffee shop make amends?'

'Far more than a serf is worth, I'm sure,' he said, with a wry smile.

CHAPTER FIVE
The road to nowhere

In the Khan el Khalili souk in the centre of Cairo, hot dust rose from the busy narrow streets. I walked through a stream of humanity, people who seemed to belong in another age or an old, long-forgotten movie. Men in long galabeyas and loose turbans wandered beside women wearing long robes and the hijab, and a few women wore the full black burqa. Rickety donkey carts laden high and wide forced the crowds to part just long enough for them to get through. An ornate glass-fronted shop selling expensive-looking gold jewellery was the neighbour of a crammed, open-fronted tailor shop where five men worked diligently on endlessly-whirring sewing machines. A mother cat and her huddle of skinny kittens sunned themselves amongst straw, grime and dried orange peel in a doorway.

'Yalla!' shouted a boy holding a metal tray high above his head. I was the only one to react and get out of his way and yet the boy expertly dodged the crowd to deliver small glasses of sweet tea to a stallholder.

Industrious clamour surrounded me. Incomprehensible conversations eluded me. Exotic smells assaulted me.

This was not the Africa I'd joined Dragoman to see, and I was about three thousand years too late to see lions here unless you counted the statues with the lioness face of Sekhmet, the warrior goddess. But Egypt seduced me from the first moment I arrived. I was captivated by its unfamiliar culture and languages, the striking desert scenery interspersed with bright green ribbons of palm trees, and, of course, its romantic and mysterious ancient history.

On my two previous trips, I'd got used to going around places mostly on my own unless it was a group excursion. Freddie tended to prefer tinkering on the truck and I kept as far away from Ryan as I could. Guy had so far given me no reason to suspect he was particularly interested in exploring the back streets of crowded souks, so it was a surprise when I spotted him in the Khan el Khalili sitting outside a small coffee shop smoking a sheesha.

'Hi!' I said. 'Mind some company?'

It was the first time we'd had a chance to sit and chat without anyone else around. At Camp Green, I'd found it hard to get a sensible conversation out of him. He was friendly enough but seemed too sure of himself and had a smart, quippy answer for everything, which had rung big warning bells to me back then. Now, though, especially since arriving in Egypt, I was seeing a different side to him and feeling much more comfortable around him.

'I was just watching,' he said after I'd sat and ordered a mint tea. 'I like to just watch the world go by and let it soak in. You see those men over there?' He pointed to two very dirty men in vests sitting cross-legged on the ground in a dirty stall crammed with old car tyres. 'Since I've been here, they've made a bucket and some soles for shoes out of those tyres. That's bloody hard work and takes real skill.'

As we were sitting, he told me some stories about when he drove from the UK to Johannesburg in a Land Rover with a friend seven years previously. They were both just twenty-two at the time. I'd known he'd done that year-long trip— he'd mentioned it more than once back in the workshop — but what I'd ungenerously taken as bragging back in Camp Green had now softened into a genuine enthusiasm for experiencing the world.

'It was a mind-blowing journey,' he said, 'but we missed a lot because we didn't do much research. We drove past things we didn't even know were there, like the gorillas in Uganda. Criminal! I saw so much and learned so much, but I also missed so much. When we came back, I got a job working in the city but after five years I realised I had to get back out on the road. That's why I'm here.'

'So you've seen most of Egypt before then?'

'I've seen a lot of it, yes, but I love Egypt and I was happy when G said I was coming here with you. I saw the highlights before, of course, but nothing in much depth. Now's my chance.'

Knowing that Guy had a real passion to explore the places we were visiting changed things for me. Here was someone who I could enthuse with about the history, the culture and the sights on our journey. Yes, I always shared things with the passengers I travelled with, but there was inevitably a different relationship there. I was working and I had responsibilities which came before having fun so I was not always able to join any of the group when they went out exploring on free time. Maybe Guy would be good company after all.

The Egyptian Museum on Cairo's Tahrir Square is the museum of the pharaohs. To walk through this palatial pink building is to time travel through thousands of years of ancient Egypt. It was the perfect starting point for our journey down the Nile Valley. In the towering ground floor halls, lofty stone pharaohs looked down their noses at the mere mortals worshipping at their feet, and majestic sphinxes sat alongside statues of hawk-headed gods. In the upper levels, royal mummies lay in glass cases far from the quiet, dark tombs of their supposedly final repose while their mummified pet cats languished in a nearby room with dogs, hawks, snakes, crocodiles and other animals embalmed for the afterlife.

In the Old Kingdom, death was the realm of the god Anubis. In a wide corridor, on top of a golden shrine, Anubis in the form of a sleek black jackal with a gold-leaf collar crouched attentively. This statue had been found guarding the inner entrance of a small, long-forgotten tomb buried in the sands of the Valley of the Kings. The tomb was that of a boy with a club foot and a crooked spine, a boy who died at the age of nineteen over 3,300 years ago, a boy who was a king — Tutankhamun.

Seeing the display of exquisite riches unearthed in Tutankhamun's tomb by Howard Carter in 1922 was like watching a fantasy version of an ancient illuminated manuscript come to life. Vivid blues of lapis lazuli and turquoise, rich orange-reds of carnelian, pearls and glass beads had all been combined with an abundance of gold by extraordinarily gifted craftsmen to make resplendent jewellery and masks fit for a king. I looked forward to seeing the faces of the group in a few days' time when they saw the unadorned poky tomb where these thousands of priceless objects were discovered.

But before we headed south, we had to explore the pyramids. When I first came here, I felt almost cheated when I realised the pyramids were so close to the city of Giza on the outskirts of Cairo. I thought they were out in the desert. Of course, they *are* in the desert, it's just that there are also settlements of over eight million people surrounding them on three sides. Get your perspective right though, and the sight of the three Giza pyramids, especially with the Sphinx in the foreground, is a sight I defy anyone to tire of. I knew some of our group would want to go inside the Great Pyramid of Cheops but I most certainly wouldn't be joining them. Once was enough. Groping along a narrow stone corridor, gasping for air and following the sweaty backside of the person in front wasn't my idea of a good morning even if it was in one of the Seven Ancient Wonders of the World. I would save my tomb raiding for the Valley of the Kings in Luxor.

The road from Cairo to Luxor was a narrow strip of liberally pot-holed tarmac that ran roughly parallel to the River Nile. For most of the way, this busy road was flanked on both sides by thin strips of gravel or sand, then fields which were generally at a lower level. You needed your wits about you to drive here and often ended up driving with the two outer wheels on the gravel when one of the many oncoming trucks decided not to give enough passing room or if you had to quickly pass a mule cart or someone on a push-bike carrying some astonishing load such as huge bags of charcoal. Go too far off the tarmac, though, and you'd slide off the road completely and finish up in the fields. Guy and I regularly swapped the driving duty so as not to tire and lose concentration.

Mid-morning of our second day, having just stopped to buy a block of ice in the town of Asyut, Guy was driving and I was half-dozing in my preferred position with my feet up on the dashboard. Talking Heads' *The Road to Nowhere* was playing on the truck stereo and the sound of chatter and laughter filtered into the cab which was open to the passenger compartment. It was hot and sunny, there were cold drinks in the coolbox, we'd had a fun night wild camping last night, and we were just half a day from Luxor. We were all happy.

BANG! No, not just bang, but bang, crash, crunch and screech! Christ!

Glass shattered, metal writhed and distorted, plastic cracked. The cab had exploded around me. I found myself lying with my feet halfway out of the now smashed windscreen which was hanging out of the front of the truck. We'd stopped. I cautiously tried to take in my immediate surroundings, unwilling to move at first. The passenger door was bent awkwardly outwards and its window was in smithereens. The floor beneath me had buckled upwards — thank God my legs hadn't been there or blood and bone would have been added to the unholy mess I was sitting in.

I looked across at Guy. He was sitting stock-still holding onto the steering wheel, looking over at me.

'Are you okay?' he said, his voice strained with concern.

'I— I'm fine, I think. Yes,' I said, mentally checking myself out, 'I'm not hurt. You?'

'I'm all right.'

Then the panic hit me — Jesus, the group. I struggled upright and turned.

'Is everyone okay?'

Shocked faces stared back at me but no-one was hurt. However bad everything else was, everyone was safe.

Guy and I picked our way out of the chaos of the cab to inspect the damage from the outside.

'The fucking idiot just ploughed straight into us, head on,' said Guy. 'He tried to overtake someone and just massively misjudged it. I slammed on the brakes but he was too close. He's in the field over there now.' He pointed to the trashed mess of a small van wrapped around a tree. Amazed, we watched the driver walk away from the vehicle.

It was disastrous for us. No windscreen and the passenger-side door of the cab was badly mangled and had no glass left. Crumpled metal wrapped itself around the front left wheel, the front of the truck and radiator were thoroughly bashed-in on one side despite the sturdy bull bar, one headlight was gone, and heaven knows what other problems lay hidden under the wreckage. We were in a bad way. Our truck was slewed across the road, blocking most of it, but still the Egyptian trucks carried on trying to squeeze past us as if it was just a normal part of the day on this section of the Nile road. Perhaps it was. Guy got out tools and tried to release the metal that was stopping the wheel from moving so we could at least push the truck to the side of the road. Before long, though, the police arrived. They had the van driver in their car.

'You come to police station. Bring passports. All passports.'

'If you want to leave the keys with me, Amanda, I'll see if I can get us to the side of the road.' Adrian was a mechanic by trade, so I accepted gratefully.

I was relieved that the senior policeman left two guards with the group.

The rest of the afternoon was an exercise in red tape and frustration. The police chief wanted to complete hand-written reports and forms about the incident — in at least triplicate — along with noting the names and passport details of all the passengers. Since we spoke no Arabic and they spoke little English, it was not easy. They were very hospitable, keeping us generously supplied with tea, but it took four excruciating hours.

At least we weren't hurt; the man-with-the-van was dealt with less kindly and his injuries left untreated.

Our companions had a stressful afternoon too, having been abandoned on the roadside in the searing heat and wondering where on earth their tour leaders had been taken. Eventually, though, we got back to the truck. Adrian had managed to move it but daylight was now beginning to fade and the police wouldn't let us go anywhere without at least a windscreen. And so it was that, after being shown where to get a new windscreen — which was unceremoniously and unconvincingly forced into the misshapen hole at the front of our cab — we ended up being given special permission to spend the night camping in the grounds of the Police Officers' Club in Asyut.

We'd started the day happily. We ended the day miserable, knackered, hot, hungry, and worried about what this all meant for the continuation of the trip. I couldn't say anything to ease everyone's concerns that night as I simply didn't know what we might be able to do with the truck and how long it would take. For now, we all just needed to eat and sleep.

This was not how I'd imagined my last Egypt and Middle East journey ending, and I felt terrible for the group.

It looked like we were on the road to nowhere.

CHAPTER SIX
I can fix this

I woke to the familiar rattle of keys and the sound of someone dragging the kitchen boxes out of the truck so they could set up for breakfast. I didn't know who was on cook duty this morning but it seemed like a very early start. I got dressed and forced myself out of my tent. The day had to be faced.

'Oh, it's you!'

Guy never got up early but here he was, cigarette in hand, getting the kettle on.

'Couldn't sleep so I thought I may as well get up,' he said, unsmiling.

We sat, Guy drinking strong black coffee and me with my black Earl Grey tea, and chatted about our options for the day. Miraculously, the truck was in safe working order as far as the engine was concerned. It seemed to be just the bodywork that was the problem, along with the lack of headlights, the precarious new windscreen, and the smashed passenger side window which meant the truck could never be left alone as we couldn't secure it.

Our friends slowly emerged and joined us for breakfast. The mood was sombre.

Halfway through breakfast, a young Egyptian man approached us rather hesitantly.

'I can fix this,' he said, simply, waving his hand at our

bedraggled truck.

One problem with being a foreign traveller in Egypt is that you attract many people who think you need whatever they're selling, that they know exactly the right route to the place you're going, and that their brother/father/mother/son have precisely the skills to help you — no matter what the issue. You start by being polite then end up reacting with anything from scepticism to dismissiveness and occasionally rudeness if they are too persistent or you've had a bad day, but rarely with appreciation since they are almost invariably mistaken.

'Thanks, mate, but we'll sort it. Shukran,' said Guy, in dismissive mode.

But the man didn't leave. He hovered silently, looking at the truck, then the ground and then at us once more. He certainly wasn't the usual pushy type.

'I can fix this with my father. We have shop in Nag Hammadi. We fix good as new. My father is expert.'

Guy and I looked at each other. We didn't have another plan. If we didn't get the truck fixed, the trip was probably at an end. Even if Dragoman had a free truck, there was no way they would be able to get one to us quickly enough to continue the trip, so all the passengers would probably have to go home. Sometimes, you just have to go with your gut and the only option that is presenting itself to you, and hope that the gods are with you.

Nag Hammadi is a small town on the way to Luxor, about a four-hour drive from Asyut. Having explained to the group that we either had to find a way to fix the truck or the trip was at an end, they all backed our decision to go and see Mustafa's father. There wasn't much choice. And so we headed cautiously down the Nile road once more.

As we drove, Guy and I made a plan. We would go to Luxor where I would stay with the group and arrange excursions to see all the sites and Guy would take the truck back to Nag Hammadi. Mustafa said it would take one day to fix the bodywork, replace the headlights and make the new windscreen more secure. We dropped Mustafa at his workshop which was down a back street littered with old cars, trucks and tyres, and agreed that Guy would return early the next morning. At Luxor campsite, we erected our large cook tent to house the cook tables, stoves and boxes full of cooking pots, utensils and staple foods. Our group decided what personal gear they wanted with them for the next day and then everything else was locked up in the secure back locker of the truck — a safer bet than leaving anything valuable in tents.

The truck was our base, our home, so it felt strangely disorientating watching Guy head off the next morning. I prayed that Mustafa was right and that they could do the work in a day, but it seemed like a big ask so Guy said he would somehow find a phone and get word to the campsite if he was unable to get back by nightfall. I thanked my lucky stars that it was Guy I was sharing this burden with and not Ryan. I had total trust in him to look after the truck and to ensure that Mustafa's team did the best job they could. It would not be an easy day for him. I, on the other hand, knew I would love exploring Luxor and the Valley of the Kings once again despite the problems. It was a privilege to show everyone the phenomenal sights they'd come to see and I was sure that everyone would soon have a smile on their face once more.

But for me, things didn't go quite as expected.

The spectacular avenue of human-headed sphinxes flanked our entrance into the vast complex of Karnak Temple. Passing colossal sandstone pylons inscribed with huge reliefs of pharaohs and gods, we were soon walking through the great Hypostyle Hall. This forest of 134 colossal pillars covered with hieroglyphs and rich imagery and topped with open papyrus blossom capitals made my heart beat faster and my soul sing. It wasn't just the desert heat seeping from the warm stone columns, it was history — four thousand years of it — and if you looked up to the corners shielded from the harsh sun, you could still see the colours which would have once covered every inch of this temple complex.

I couldn't begin to understand how you could be left unmoved by all this, and yet many of the group were fractious and grumpy. It was as if they'd decided the trip was doomed and there was no point enjoying themselves. I felt like a teacher dragging around a group of thirteen-year-olds on a school geography trip.

'Oh, buck up and get a life. Just look at where you are. You're walking in the footsteps of pharaohs on the banks of the Nile, for God's sake. You're touching ancient history. This is what you came for.'

Maybe that's what I should have said but I was still a long way off having the kind of confidence I'd have needed for that. Instead, that afternoon, I tried to cheer them up by paying for them to use a swimming pool at a posh hotel in town and, later, bought them all dinner in a restaurant. The mood did lighten somewhat, but when we got back to the campsite and heard the news that Guy would not be returning that day, humours flattened once again. Perhaps tomorrow's trip to the Valley of the Kings would bring them round.

If you have even the slightest romantic disposition, it requires no effort to imagine being an explorer of old as you trek through the desert sands of the Valley of the Kings and the nearby Valley of the Queens. You are one mirage away from being Howard Carter and you could easily conjure up Indiana Jones arriving on horseback through the dusty heat haze. History literally lies beneath your feet and the urge to start digging with the archaeologists can be surprisingly tempting. The valley is on the west bank of the Nile and it is the last resting place of pharaohs, queens, high priests and other elites of Egypt's New Kingdom of about three thousand five hundred to three thousand years ago. The great and the good were entombed here as mummies in chambers hidden in the nothingness of this barren stretch of desert, along with a staggering array of goods they might need in the afterlife.

The thrill of discovering a tomb must be heart-stoppingly exciting. Even as a visitor it is spine-tingling to enter a nondescript-looking stone doorway to a roughly hewn corridor which becomes more refined as it disappears into the hillside. A few of the tombs are small and sparsely decorated — Tutankhamun's is a surprising example — but others are cavernous underground rock palaces with high ceilings, carved columns and multiple rooms, some still housing the sarcophagus of the buried dignitary or royal personage. The decoration is often simply jaw-dropping — every surface covered in paintings of gods, pharaohs, animals, armies, hieroglyphs . . . All life is pictured here and the works of art could have been finished just yesterday so vivid are the dark blue ceilings glittering with white stars, the red dresses of goddesses and the blue-green waters of the Nile carrying golden barges. Three and a half thousand years after being painted, the scenes had the power to speak to people living in a different world far from anything the artists could have comprehended, so perhaps the dreams of everlasting life for the occupants and makers of the tombs were not as unrealistic as we might imagine.

Thankfully, the valley worked its magic and the morning was a success but the early afternoon brought yet more challenges. The day's cook group returned from the market without any food.

'There's no decent food at all. Everything's got flies on it. It's disgusting.'

The muttering and moaning started again. Wow, they really had hit the doldrums. I certainly hadn't counted on a mutiny. Is it a mutiny when your cook team refuses to buy food and cook for the group? It felt like it.

Right, there was nothing else for it, I had to get them out of this negative frame of mind they were all in. I was their tour leader so it was up to me. I had to step up to the plate. Drawing on my northern pragmatism, I could see something needed to be done so I would try to make it happen. I didn't have musical abilities to fall back on to cheer them up, nor did I feel able to laugh and joke them back into a good frame of mind. I decided my weapon of choice in this battle would have to be food. My mum was an excellent cook and I'd learned a thing or two from her.

Through a contact at a hotel, I arranged for a case of beers to be brought to the campsite. Then I grabbed the shopping bags and a willing helper in the form of Will, the ever-cheerful Dutchman, and headed to the market. We managed to find an ice-seller and bought a huge chunk of ice from a dark, straw-filled hole in the ground, which I asked to be delivered to camp. We then bought enough food for a feast from the wonderful produce on offer. Yes, there were flies, this was Egypt and it was hot, of course there were flies — carcasses that were hung from hooks or displayed on open counters were covered in flies despite the butcher's occasional swatting efforts. But the smell, or lack thereof, told me the meat was fresh, and with proper cooking, there was no way anyone was going to get sick on my watch. As for the fruit and vegetables, we had bright purple potassium permanganate to wash everything in, so again, no issues. I had to remember that I was used to this now but the group wasn't, not yet. I had to show them what could be done.

Back at camp, I cooked up a storm. Chicken with herbs, olives and lemons, along with rice, a gorgeous tomato salad and flatbreads, followed by sliced oranges with honey and cinnamon. It went down a treat, especially with the cold beers, and we actually managed to have a good evening with some smiles and laughter for a change.

By the time nine o'clock came round, all the conversation was about when Guy might be coming back with the truck and what might have happened to him. I hadn't had any more messages so I assumed he was on his way, but I had no real clue. There could have been any amount of reasons why he wasn't here yet, and it was still possible he might not turn up. But I was now getting concerned about him. Was he all right? Had something awful happened to him? By eleven o'clock, we all gave in and went to bed. He obviously wasn't coming tonight. Please God let him be safe.

It was the exhaust brake I heard first. I didn't wear a watch so I didn't know the time. I could have been asleep for minutes or hours but it was still pitch black. Was I dreaming? No, I knew the sounds of our truck. I threw on some clothes and clambered out of my tent to meet Guy as he parked up by the cook tent. A few tent zips were opened and sleepy but smiling faces peered out.

I don't think Guy was expecting a big hug and kiss on the

cheek but I was just so happy to see him. He looked totally knackered and utterly filthy. I wanted to ask so much but at that dark, unknown hour the conversation was very limited.

'Are you all right?' I asked.

'Yeah, I'm fine.'

'Do you need food?'

'No.'

'A cuppa?'

'No. Thanks. I just need to sleep,' he said, hardly able to keep his eyes open.

'Take my tent,' I said, 'We didn't put one up for you 'cos we didn't think you were going to make it.'

'No, I'll just sleep here by the truck. It's still not secure — no side window. Speak in the morning, yeah?'

I left him rolling out his sleeping mat and bag onto the ground at the other side of the truck to our tents, and went back to bed. Relief brought sleep quickly.

'What the hell—? For fuck's sake.' An infuriated voice rang out around the camp in the early morning light.

Oh for crying out loud, what now?

Dressing hastily, I got up to see what was going on. The once dust-dry earth around the truck was now sodden. What the heck had happened? I went round to see Guy as the others got up to investigate too.

Guy was marooned in his sleeping bag in a huge lake of water. He was sitting up, obviously not yet fully awake, trying to comprehend his predicament. A campsite groundsman must have left a tap on overnight by mistake. Within a minute, nearly the whole group stood staring silently at Guy, not quite sure what to do or say.

Then, quietly and looking a bit confused, he said, 'I thought I'd wet myself.'

Never has true side-splitting laughter been so welcome. We laughed till we cried.

'I'm glad you all find this so funny,' he said and stood up leaving a puddle of soggy sleeping bag around his feet. He stood there in his boxers and shouted, 'Well, don't just stand there. Bring me coffee!'

He got coffee. We laughed. We ate breakfast. We chatted happily. We packed up and got in the truck to leave, then we got out again — the truck was stuck in the waterlogged ground. We laughed. We all pushed the truck and got ridiculously muddy. We thought it was hysterical. How moods can change in an instant. All the negativity was gone, our happy friends were back to normal and, from that moment on, I just knew this was going to turn out to be a very special trip.

CHAPTER SEVEN
Aladdin & Ozymandias

Aswan. Once seen, never forgotten. Golden sand dunes drop down to the silvery-blue waters of the Nile which flows past time-worn granite boulders. Here and there the river is edged with the complementary greens of papyrus and palms and dotted with the white sails of feluccas. On an evening, this striking scene is suffused with an exotic, spicy amber glow lending it an air of antique mystery and magic.

The very best spot on the eastern riverbank — a vast black granite bluff overlooking this unique panorama — was bagged in 1898 by the Old Cataract Hotel. Drawing upper-class adventurers from around the world with its attractive Moorish architecture and luxurious service, the hotel became a notable feature of the town and, despite its fortunes waxing and waning over the years, it remained the place to aspire to for many visitors to Aswan. Sadly, our kitty didn't quite reach to a stay in the Old Cataract, but Aswan campsite was about as attractive a place as you could wish for, set next to sand dunes overlooking the river.

As soon as we arrived I sent out word that I was looking for Aladdin — emphasis on the last syllable and pronounced more like *Alladeen*, if you'd be so kind since if it's said the way most westerners pronounce it, the name just brings to mind a cartoon character. *My* Aladdin was a Nubian man who lived on Aswan's famous Elephantine Island, so-called because of the roughly elephant-shaped boulder. The Nubian people originated from southern Egypt and northern Sudan and their dark skin is testament to their links to sub-Saharan Africa. Sadly, in the 1970s when the Aswan High Dam was built just south of the town, a vast stretch of land about ten miles wide by three hundred miles long was inundated by the reservoir, Lake Nasser, and tens of thousands of Nubians were displaced from their ancestral lands. The dam also adversely affected the flooding of the Nile so fertility in the Nile Valley has been dropping ever since. There are, of course, also positive arguments for the dam (electricity, reliable water provision, no crocodiles), but I wish we could work *with* rather than against nature more often.

Aladdin was a softly spoken, ever-smiling man who arranged sailing trips in the feluccas he owned, including visiting the west bank and island sights of the Aga Khan's mausoleum, Elephantine Island and the ancient Nilometer. The second time I met him, Aladdin had stolen a little piece of my heart. Having astutely guessed that I was having a bad time with Ryan, he offered to take me out for a late afternoon felucca ride. At one point, in the middle of the Nile, he got a long length of rope which was tied to the back of the boat and threw the end in the river, saying, 'OK, now is your time to be happy.'

'I am happy, Aladdin. I'm loving this. Thank you.'

'Good, but not as happy as you will be, believe me. Get in.'

'What?! No!'

'Yes, trust me, I do it lots of times.'

He cajoled and encouraged me until I gave in and jumped in the water wearing my shorts and t-shirt. It was colder than I expected but I warmed quickly.

'Are you swimming too?' I called.

'No,' he said, laughing, 'I have to sail. Grab the rope.'

'You're joking?'

He wasn't. He set sail and off we went, the little felucca

pulling me gently through the waters of the Nile. He was right, I was immediately and deliciously happy. Trying to avoid taking mouthfuls of river, I laughed and whooped like an idiot, and I could hear Aladdin giggling in the felucca. What a gift! And from a man I'd only met once before. Friendship is a funny thing. You can know someone for years and never really get past that acquaintance stage, or you can meet someone from the other side of the world just once and feel a bond. Aladdin was a friend, and I was delighted to see him again when he arrived at the campsite.

'Ah, merhaba, Amanda. I see that your swim in the Nile made sure that you came back to Egypt.'

'Egyptian sorcery, my friend. I didn't realise you were a Nubian witch!'

I decided that I should stay behind with our unlockable truck and let Guy head out with the group on all the excursions, including the Philae Temple and the fascinating Unfinished Obelisk. We would all meet up later for a G&T in the bar at the Old Cataract. Well, you can pretend for an evening!

Guy most definitely deserved a day exploring with Aladdin after the two dreadful days he'd ended up having in Nag Hammadi.

'Mustafa and his dad hugely underestimated how long the job would take them,' Guy had explained when we were driving from Luxor to Aswan. 'Bloody hell, they are workers, though. And with so few tools — they didn't even own a chisel! They just kept taking crumpled bits of metal off the truck and then hammering the hell out of them for hour after hour til they knackered themselves. There was no workshop, no shade. It was all happening in the street and there was filth everywhere.'

'Gosh, you must have fried,' I said.

'You could say. And there was a slaughterhouse over the road. The stench and the flies were unbelievable. By about midday, I

53

felt like shit and my stomach was turning somersaults but I couldn't leave the truck 'cos there were so many kids around and they kept trying to nick stuff from our toolbox.'

'Was there a loo?'

'I'd rather not think about that, thanks.'

'Ah, like that?'

'Oh yes, and worse. But Mustafa's family were all really kind. When we knew the work wasn't going to be finished on that first day, Mustafa took me back to their one-room house. His mother had made us beans, rice and chicken for dinner. I was so embarrassed 'cos I could see they had very little and they were so generous in sharing their food but I was crippled with stomach pains and couldn't eat much.'

'Did you sleep there?'

'Sleep? No. After dinner we went back to the truck and work carried on. Honestly, they didn't stop until the muezzin called out at 4 a.m. I grabbed a couple of hours in the truck at that point. I just couldn't stay awake any longer.'

Work had carried on frantically all the next day with Guy watching heart in mouth as they slowly pieced the truck back together again. Despite them not managing to get glass for the cab's passenger window, Guy knew he had to leave that day.

'It was an unbelievably skilled piece of work they did. They were brilliant guys. I know if I'd given them another day, it would have been near perfect but I couldn't leave you guys for another night. I left it as late as I could, paid them well, then left. And I don't want to do that again, ever,' he added.

'Okay, so we'll agree not to crash the truck again, eh?'

'Yeah, all right then.'

I'd have loved to stretch our stay in Aswan to a second day but it just wasn't possible. Places to go, people to see, temples to visit. And the next temple was a bit special. Of course, they're all special in their own way but this one was rather different. The two huge rock temples at Abu Simbel were built for Ramses II, the pharaoh also known as Ozymandias, the 'King of Kings' seen by that 'traveller from an antique land' in Shelley's famous poem. The poem tells of the towering statue of a once-powerful pharaoh reduced to two legs and a crumbling head in the desert sands. This mighty king has not fallen as badly as some, though, since his Abu Simbel temples, an incredible feat of construction in their day (1244 BC), became the focus of a second remarkable engineering project which saved them from obscurity over three thousand years later in 1968. Lake Nasser, the reservoir made by the Aswan High Dam, was going to drown Ramses' temples, so the decision was made to cut the temples out of the rock face they were carved into and move them to higher ground. Block by block they were made into gigantic 'Lego' bricks and then rebuilt within a man-made concrete mountain. They were even carefully positioned to take account of the fact that the opening to the great temple would have been illuminated by the rising sun on two important days of the year: Ramses' birthday and his coronation day — or so it's believed, and I like the story. I also like the fact that we cared enough about our history and culture to put this amount of effort and money into such a project. We are definitely the richer for it and I'm sure Ramses II would have expected no less.

After crossing the dam, the road from Aswan heads south on the west side of Lake Nasser until it reaches Abu Simbel, just before the Sudanese border. It was about a four-hour drive for our truck. There is nothing, nothing at all, except road and sand between the dam and the turnoff to the temples. Ever since we'd arrived in Egypt the temperature had been steadily rising and the day we drove from Aswan to Abu Simbel it was a staggering forty-eight degrees celsius — as hot as hell. With the window glass in the passenger side of the cab still missing, it was like driving whilst being blasted by a huge hairdryer. I'd taken the first hour's drive and Guy was coming close to the end of his first hour-long stint at the wheel.

'I'm getting tired, Amanda. I'm going to pull over at that service station coming up, all right?'

I looked at him. He had a slightly odd look in his eyes.

'Okay,' I said. 'Maybe just pull up right now, eh?'

'It's all right,' he said, 'I'll get to the garage.'

'Guy, there is no service station.'

He turned his head sharply in my direction.

'Really? I figured the lakes weren't real, but the fuel station too?'

'Mhm.'

Our friends were taking no chances after hearing that little episode, so for the last two hours of the journey they tried to keep us cool by draping our head and shoulders with towels dampened with cold water from the coolbox. I thought at the time that that would be the toughest journey I'd ever undertake. Hah!

We explored the magnificent temples in the afternoon then, after a hot night in the desert and another short early morning visit, we returned to Aswan. Thank goodness the glass we'd ordered for the side window was ready and waiting for us. At last, our truck was secure once again and we wouldn't have to be desiccated by another 'fan oven' drive like the two we'd just endured. We were back in control and ready to head through the Sinai Peninsula over the next few days and then across the Red Sea to Jordan.

CHAPTER EIGHT
Adventures in Jordan

Jordan, or to give it its formal name, the Hashemite Kingdom of Jordan, is a small Arab country sandwiched between Israel, Palestine, Saudi Arabia, Iraq and Syria. Barring a tiny sixteen-mile stretch of Red Sea coast, it is land-locked — the Dead Sea on the country's western border doesn't really count. Unusually in this corner of the world, this little kingdom is stable, its people well-educated, and its monarchy and government committed to peace. Unless you're an Islamic extremist who abhors the country's peace treaty with Israel and good relations with the west, Jordan is a good neighbour that welcomes outsiders, causes little to no upset, and never has stupidly loud parties — though they do like a good meal and a sing-song round a campfire.

Even if you know nothing about Jordan, you've probably heard of Wadi Rum if you've watched the iconic movie '*Lawrence of Arabia*'. Wadi Rum is the desert valley from where British officer, T.E.Lawrence, made his successful surprise attack against the Ottoman Empire in Aqaba in 1917. Up until the last century, tens or even hundreds of thousands of Bedouins lived a nomadic lifestyle in this vast, arid landscape, and you can still see ancient rock art here. In this unforgiving terrain, tribal tensions could often escalate into bloody feuds so, in 1931, a new paramilitary force was set up to control the region. The Desert Patrol is made up of members taken mostly from local Bedouin tribes. One sandy valley flanked by red sandstone mountains and granite rocks would be indistinguishable from another for most incomers, and an understanding of tribal sensitivities is vital for the job. I'm sure these well-trained law enforcers do a great job, but on a purely superficial level, boy, they certainly know how to cut a dash in their uniforms! Long khaki robes with thick red leather belts attached to crossed red bandoleers for ammunition, a silver dagger holstered at their waist and a scarf headdress of the traditional red-and-white checkered keffiyeh. Sadly, they often prefer 4x4s to their hump-backed friends these days but even without the added accoutrement of a camel, the effect is still masterful. The Desert Patrol is an indisputable force working in inhospitable lands, though these days the men are less concerned with potentially deadly tribal arguments and more often used as a stylish rescue service for lost or injured tourists, as well as keeping a firm eye on any would-be smugglers passing through their wadis.

As you get close to Wadi Rum, a single-track railway line crosses the road. A train was passing as we drove up to the crossing point. It was going very slowly, and then, as we waited for it to pass, it ground to a halt. Weirdly, it then started shunting backwards. Great! A train playing silly buggers in the middle of the desert. Just what we needed. The train driver eventually drew his engine level to us, then got out and came over to see us.

'Salam wa alaykum,' he said, as he stepped on the foothold and pulled himself up by the wing mirror to talk to me. He had a broad grin on his face.

'Wa alaykum salam,' I replied, wishing for the umpteenth time that my knowledge of Arabic didn't end more or less there.

I expected him to want something or have a question, but he

just smiled at me and Guy and peered around to our friends in the back and waved. It seemed this was a social call. We managed to pass the time of day for about ten minutes with his broken English and lots of sign language, then he waved goodbye, got back in his engine and set off again. This charming fellow obviously didn't see many people as a rule so thought nothing of backing his train up for a quick 'hello'.

I hadn't expected the same affability from the Desert Patrol, but we must have been a particularly friendly-looking bunch that day as, when we reached the patrol station at the entrance to the wadi, we were all invited for tea. Bedouins are some of the most sociable and friendly people you will find, and, in common with many others who live in harsh terrains, will share anything they have if you need it. But really, inviting fifteen overlanders for tea?!

The trip into Wadi Rum was thrilling for two reasons: the stunning desert scenery and sand-matting. On the side of Dragoman trucks we carried up to four lengths of steel about one-and-a-half by half a metre, each with three rows of large holes. These were ex-army items and overlanders called them either sand mats or mud mats depending on the terrain being crossed. Driving a sixteen-ton truck across soft sand requires a bit of skill which can only come from practice. Just before we entered the wadi, I deflated the tyres so we had more surface area and were less likely to sink, but I knew it was almost guaranteed that we would end up with wheels buried in the sand at some point. Actually, this was half the fun as long as it didn't go on too long, and this was where sand-matting came in.

'Okay, everybody out!' I shouted, as we gently sank to an inevitable halt.

The sand mats were unbolted from the truck and we got out

the shovels from the tool locker. The idea is to get as much of the soft sand away from the wheels as possible, then try to wedge the mats in front of the back wheels so the truck can then get purchase on the hard metal and extricate itself simply and elegantly from the grip of the desert. As you can probably imagine, it's easier said than done, plus, one wrong move with a truck and people digging around wheels and huge chunks of metal which could fly out if badly placed . . . well, you just wouldn't want to think about it.

Between us all, we crawled under the truck and dug and positioned sand mats. After a few failed attempts, we got some momentum going and everyone dashed to the back of the truck to start pushing to keep it moving. It was hard work and some people ate a lot of sand, but it was a good laugh and we hoped we'd got some great photos to prove that we'd been there and done that.

By the evening, we'd spent most of the day exploring and having fun in the wadi. We had a barbecue night under the stars and most of us didn't bother with tents but just slept out by the campfire in the middle of this river of red sand hemmed in by time-worn crags. When the exuberance of the group eventually died down, a stillness descended on the wadi. At first, the mountains were just dark formations blocking the stars' descent to the desert sands, but the moon was rising and soon one side of the wadi was illuminated in its cooling light. A warm breeze ruffled and rippled the surface of the desert with a gentle shhh.

'This is a bit special, isn't it?' I whispered to Guy, who had put his sleeping bag just a little way from mine.

'Probably even more special than we realise,' he said. 'Night.'

An unpleasantly crammed ferry ride across the Red Sea from Egypt's Sinai Peninsula had brought us to Jordan a couple of days earlier. We landed at Jordan's only port town, Aqaba. By then, a sense of normality had taken hold of the group. We had our daily rhythm of packing and unpacking, shopping, cooking lunch and dinner, singing along to songs on tapes while driving and with Pete and Guy on guitars on many an evening, and of course, exploring each place we came to. Everyone was having fun, including me. Since Aswan, I'd noticed that Guy was very happy to stick with me and share either any required work on the truck or any exploring that was to be had. We were enjoying each other's company.

Having finalised the Jordanian border formalities and then got the camp set up at Aqaba, Guy suggested we have a night off. That was a novel thought. I'd not done that on either of my other trips and it felt almost naughty — as if we were Mum and Dad leaving the kids to fend for themselves. At Alibaba's restaurant in Aqaba town, we had the most delicious meal I'd had for a long time. We shared a platter of garlic prawns followed by chateaubriand steak and salad, all washed down with a teapot of lager — an actual teapot as they couldn't legally serve alcohol. For people earning just £6 a day it was a major extravagance but it was worth every penny and we returned home to our tents stuffed and happy.

I might only be small — my dad always described me as being 'no bigger than a minute' — but I love my food. That evening, I discovered that Guy was a bit of a foodie too. Oddly, even now, I often remember a time and a place by recalling a particularly good or interesting meal. For me, food is like music or smells in that it can easily bring me back to a moment. On this trip, the meal in

Aqaba would be the first of four food-related moments to strike a chord. Unexpectedly, all four chords turned out to be Guy-shaped. Finding a friendship with Guy was making this trip a particularly happy one for me, but I definitely wasn't looking for any deeper connection with him. He was someone to share the job with and have a laugh with for eight weeks, then he'd go his way (probably a repeat of this trip but as the leader) and I'd go mine (hopefully on the six-month long trans-Africa trip I had my heart set on). I had someone I cared for back in the UK, though admittedly, I still wasn't sure where things were going with Andy. Guy isn't my type, I told myself, and I'm certainly not his.

The two main highlights of our last few days in Jordan were the rose-red city of Petra and the exceptional Roman ruins of Jerash. At Jerash, Jen, Dave, Tom, Will and I all danced the can-can on the stage of the uncannily intact North Theatre, feeling a lot like we were just filling in at the interval while the real players changed costume and the toga-clad audience got their ice creams. The whole of this vast ancient city gives the impression of holding its breath for the imminent return of its recently departed inhabitants. Bedraggled it might be, but the remnants still show a city that you could imagine being full of life. Time-worn ruts in the stone roads tell of thousands of wooden carts and leather-clad feet passing the ornate columns on the way to the oval forum, or of the populace heading to the hippodrome to watch Ben Hur. But we had the city almost to ourselves and communed only with the ghosts of Romans past.

In Petra, history has a different weight and texture. Here, instead of being able to imagine life happening all around you in a similar fashion to today, you feel worlds away from anything familiar. It feels clandestine, almost dangerous, bordering on alien. You could be forgiven for thinking you'd stumbled onto a film set for a Star Wars movie, and you'll not be surprised to learn that Indiana Jones had his last crusade here. Remember the bit where he gallops down a narrow rock canyon? That's the Siq, the cleverly hidden, almost mile-long entrance to this implausibly crazy city of Nabataean traders whose buildings were carved into the rose-coloured rock faces of the mountains, and who created an ingenious water conduit system that was also carved into the rock. There might have been desert all around them but Petra would have been a hidden oasis. The Nabataeans kept control from about 300BC until about 100AD when the Romans decided they fancied a rock city of their own. No ifs, no buts, they took what they wanted. Of course they did; they had the power, they used it. And abused it.

Having said goodbye to Jordan, we drove to the border of Syria. A surly-faced official came to the passenger-side window of the cab. It was a common mistake since we were a right-hand-drive truck in mainly left-hand-drive countries.

'Who is driving this truck?' he said. It was funny to be met with almost the same question we'd been asked at the port when we entered Egypt about three weeks earlier.

I smiled and waved from behind the wheel.

'That's me. Sorry, wrong side, I know.'

The man didn't look at me, didn't acknowledge that I'd spoken. Instead, he said again, 'Who is driving this truck?'

This time Guy tried to explain. The man listened but didn't move. He waited for a moment, looked at his clipboard, then said again, quietly, 'Who is driving this truck?'

Ah, right. It dawned on us both that this was something a little deeper than a stupid border guard. The man simply couldn't accept that a woman was driving this truck. In fact, he *wouldn't* accept it. And, since he was our way into the country, he didn't have to. The power was all his. Guy and I swapped seats and the man moved over to the driver's side to begin the formalities.

No-one had hurt me and I was in no danger, but it was the first time I'd personally come across this kind of blatant misogyny and, despite understanding that I was in a different land with different customs and sensitivities, to have my presence denied in such a way felt like a kind of attack. I tried not to show it but I was shaking inside with — what? Anger? Frustration? I didn't know, but I didn't like it.

We all need a bit of power in our lives, don't we? But not the negative kind which belittles people or hurts or manipulates them — or steals their rock city! The power most of us are searching for is a positive force that allows us to be the best people we can be. We look for inner strength and confidence which hopefully shows itself kindly, as generosity and humanity. We don't always know we're hunting for such self-realisation but then, one day, if we're lucky, we look back and discover that we feel happy in our bones because we no longer have anything to prove to anyone else and we see that a gentle self-belief has settled lightly yet comfortably within us. At twenty-six, I still had a way to go. The search for my inner lioness was taking me on an unexpectedly long and unfamiliar road far from home but, oddly, it felt like it might be heading in the right direction.

CHAPTER NINE
Food for thought

A wide man on a skinny grey donkey was approaching us at a trot. There really wasn't anywhere for us to go other than into one of the stalls lining the covered street as the route was already mostly blocked by a wooden wheelbarrow piled high with fabrics.

'Welcome!' said the stall holder, clearly delighted to find himself unexpectedly visited by two tourists. The tiny stall turned out to be a restaurant — well, it sold food. 'Restaurant' was probably too grand a title for this place. The man beamed. This was obviously a God-given opportunity to sell and who was he to throw that back in the face of Allah?

'Sit, sit,' he said, all but forcing us onto two small metal chairs which might once have been blue but probably didn't ever remember being clean. Fingers snapped and two glasses of tea arrived as if conjured. Knives and forks and paper napkins appeared swiftly behind them.

'You will eat?' It wasn't really a question. 'We have roast chicken. Best chicken.' He did that Italian thing of kissing his fingertips to make sure we understood how good his chicken was.

Guy and I looked around. The stall was very narrow, as many in this souk were, but it went quite far back. Electric wires were draped in a disturbingly random manner along the walls and up to the barrel-vaulted ceiling. The heat from the oven at the back was quite intense, and so was the smell. They did indeed have chicken and now we thought about it, we were ravenous.

We were in Aleppo, a sprawling historic trading city in northern Syria, and another of my favourite places. History, mystery, souks and hammams, that's what Aleppo meant to me. In the middle of this vast city of higgledy-piggledy streets, an ancient citadel — one of the world's largest and oldest castles — rises imperiously from its limestone hill. The hill has been inhabited for five thousand years but the ruins we see now were mainly constructed in the twelfth and thirteenth centuries, the bloody time of the crusades. The history of the citadel is a fascinating saga, but the many stories behind the honeycomb of streets at its feet are just as enthralling and everyone here has a tale to tell. *This* family began buying spices from India and silks from Persia back in the sixteenth century; *his* ancestors built the great Khan al-Wazir caravanserai in the seventeenth century; *her* family helped build the Hammam al-Nahhasin; *he* makes the best roast chicken in the city.

From a distance, to the unknowing eye, this city might have looked like a nightmare of hastily thrown-up buildings caught in a cobweb of electrical wiring, but such a view would have completely missed the social vitality, cultural wealth and hidden architectural gems of the place. In the old walled quarter of the town there was a bewildering labyrinth of souks which went on for mile after mile. There was not one souk here, there were forty-five — a souk for nearly everything you could wish for: cotton, wool, soap, fur, meat, clothes, leather, jewellery, vegetables, and spices . . . I fancied you could always smell spices here no matter which souk you were in, or was that just my imagination? Having travelled through Egypt, Jordan, Syria and

Turkey twice already now, I'd seen a fair few souks, but none made my spine tingle as much as this one. I particularly loved the smaller, less grand souks which had square portals in the low arched roofs allowing restricted entry to the sun. Smoky columns of illuminated dust ended in puddles of filtered brightness on the dark streets below. You could see these shafts of light marking the passage of the covered street, and men, women and donkeys bustling along with their everyday life occasionally hit the spotlight then moved on into the obscurity of the souk. It was a timeless scene. I loved it.

Arched fronts of shops, stalls and cafes lined each side of the street but, from time to time, you would also see mysterious doorways. These were often the key to hidden places of refuge from the hustle and bustle: mosques, lodgings, hammams. We had spent that morning with the group in one of these hammams. Taking over the whole place for a couple of hours was bliss. A hammam was a tonic for mind and body. It should have been mainly for the body but we laughed so much that morning that it was an all-round therapy session. At least it was for the girls, I don't know about the boys as we were kept separate. The hammam we chose was a beautiful place to spend time in. The circular main room had a large domed stone ceiling with round and star-shaped holes letting in a gentle light. Everything other than the ceiling was warm marble including the floor and a huge table which was just on the right side of too hot. There were four recesses where you could wash in small pools which were fed by warm-water taps. Of course, you couldn't not have a water fight. I mean what else were those small bronze bowls there for? With no-one to upset or bother, and having totally drenched the place, we then ended up propelling ourselves on our bellies in races backwards and forwards across the wet marble floor, laughing hysterically. Such children. Such fun! And then the washer woman arrived. Crikey, she was big. One by one she laid us out on the hot marble slab and washed every inch of us red raw in a cloud of soap suds which did nothing to hide the scouring pad she used to relieve us of our top layer of skin. We'd each thought we had a decent tan. Turned out we were mucky.

We left the hammam tingling with a strange mix of vitality and zinginess coupled with a desire to be laid down on a feather bed and fanned whilst falling into a sleepy oblivion. However, Guy and I had discovered a perfect alternative: stuffing our faces with a shared whole chicken delivered on a bit of paper and a flatbread and with the most scrumptiously delicious lemon and garlic sauce I've ever tasted. Knives and forks? Pah! Greasy fingers and chins? Who cared!

'This is so good it's almost wrong,' said Guy. 'Thanks for sharing it with me. The company makes it even better. Cheers!'

We toasted our happy gluttony — my second memorable foodie moment with Guy — with more tea before heading back to the truck.

The third of the food incidents I came to associate with Guy happened as we were crossing the Syria-Turkey border. Just before we hit the border, I'd spent my last few Syrian pounds on a bag of strawberries. I hadn't had strawberries for ages and was chuffed to have found them. I left the bag on the dashboard as we went through all the border formalities. Even though I was driving, we had none of the issues leaving Syria that we did on entering, and in my experience so far Turkey was usually a fairly painless border. On this occasion, our Turkish border guard was a large man and I guessed he was quite high up the ranking; the fatter ones usually were. He gave us no particular grief over anything but he was ridiculously slow and made his men check on every aspect of the truck. I knew that he was looking to slow us down, probably in the hope of being given a backhander to speed things up. I didn't. I never did. I couldn't stand corruption and this man reeked of making money from his position of power. We had nothing to hide and, boring as this was, we were in no special hurry. He decided to get into the cab on the driver's side since I was out of the truck. That was unusual, but hey, whatever. He looked through our black box where we kept all our paperwork and cash tin, and just generally checked the place out. Guy looked on from the passenger seat and I stood in the doorway watching him too. By now, I knew he'd realised he wasn't going to be able to find anything he could earn 'a little extra' on. Then he spotted my paper bag of strawberries on the dash. He helped himself . . . and again. I couldn't stop myself.

'Oi! They're *my* fucking strawberries!'

Guy put his head in his hands.

The official looked down at me, possibly a little surprised, then silently turned and took another from the bag before leaving the cab with a dismissive wave of the hand to let us go.

'Really?' Guy said, as I climbed back into my seat. 'They're my fucking strawberries? I can't believe you said that! You were so lucky to get away with it.'

Nothing much seemed to shock Guy, so I found it quite funny that he was so disturbed by the incident. But it also made me realise that I'd perhaps taken a bit of a risk with my unaccustomed, badly-timed bolshiness — well, no, I knew I had, but it came out before I could stop it. I'd really not liked that man. In some ways he was worse than the Syrian border guard who wouldn't acknowledge me. *That* man had not been able to deal with me most likely due to the culture he was brought up in, but I knew that *this* man was just a corrupt official and a bully on the make. No excuses.

'Well, they *were* mine!' I said, as I put the truck in gear and we headed off into Turkey. 'He can bugger off and buy his own.'

In hindsight, I was aware that the incident could have backfired on me and I should have had more control, so it was perhaps a misplaced feeling but I was just a teensy bit pleased with myself for speaking out. Had I upset Guy, though? I looked across at him just as he looked over at me. I bit my bottom lip and grimaced. Guy couldn't keep up a serious face for long and we both melted with laughter. I had to pull over to the side of the road so I could wipe away the tears. Guy grabbed my bag of strawberries and looked back at the group.

'Strawberry anyone?'

We had two weeks planned in Turkey before our final few days crossing Europe back to the UK. Turkey was always good fun. It had a more relaxed ambience than the other countries we'd been through — tourists were not always seen as a target for an income, there was less chaos than Egypt and it felt less threatening than Syria's police state. Since our stay here also included time on the beach, it was the more holiday-like section of the trip. Before hitting the coast, though, we drove north-west up to the semi-arid Cappadocia region roughly in the centre of the country. The last time I'd been here it had been winter and the unique volcanic landscape was topped with a layer of snow. This time, the rocky valley was like a clay oven. We baked.

In around 700BC, this was a pretty dangerous place to live as you couldn't class yourself as a serious empire-builder if you hadn't had a go at Cappadocia. Over the years they were all at it — the Persians, Alexander the Great, the Romans (of course), the Seljuks — and because of this and a happy twist of geological fate, the population here became expert cave dwellers. Millions of years ago, the land here was covered in a layer of volcanic ash which hardened into rock of varying colours from white and beige to yellow and pink. This was called tuff though it was anything but tough. The soft tuff (bear with me) was then covered in a layer of tough stuff called basalt. The pale tuff eroded far more quickly than the cap of dark basalt which, by the time we got there, meant the area was a strange landscape of weird formations including some which were like tall anthills with mushroom caps balancing on top and others which were positively phallic. They are fondly known as fairy chimneys. In fact, the rocks are all different shapes and sizes as you'd expect with the carving having been left to the vagaries of rain, wind and snow for millennia, but the key thing is that humans discovered that it was much easier to dig into the rock rather than build from it and so there are thousands of cave dwellings here. Not only that, but for particularly dangerous times, they built a warren of underground cities. These are staggering feats of excavation, some with up to four levels and capable of housing up to twenty thousand people plus their livestock. Imagine, a whole city underground — it's the stuff of fantasy for most of us, but real life happened here. There were churches, schools, kitchens, stables, food cellars and tunnels . . . a lot of tunnels.

After a day's exploration, I decided to arrange a night out for us all. Dinner, music, and no doubt a little dancing in one of the cave restaurants. Our group was always up for a party and the guys at this restaurant knew how to throw one. Rowdy was probably an understatement for that night, but at least in a cave you're hardly likely to disturb the neighbours. Far too many Efes beers were drunk, some wonderful food was eaten, and, yes, music and dancing ensued. Even Guy danced, which was probably only the second time I'd seen him do that. It was a joyous night of pure abandonment as we all enjoyed making each other laugh, dancing together and singing raucously. As we left late that night, it was quite a shock to find that an unexpected storm had blown up and the rain was lashing down. Back at the camp, most of the tents had survived, thank goodness. All but mine. Like a rooky idiot, I'd left the front zip undone. My sleeping bag was drenched. You had to laugh. Well, you did in the state we were in.

'I think you might need to share a tent tonight. Want to share mine?' said Guy.

As I said before, I had no intention of getting involved with Guy. His unexpected invitation set off a beer-muddled internal monologue.

'I've got Andy back in the UK.'

Yes, but you seem to be more like friends than anything else these days.

'Guy's not my type.'

He is good-looking and has lovely hands.

'He's a driver. He'll be off with someone else on the next trip.'

He makes you smile and you like sharing experiences with him.

'He smokes far too much and I can't stand smoking.'

Funny how you put up with it from him and even learned to hand roll his cigarettes for when he's driving.

'He's arrogant.'

Well, yes, he can be but there is a much softer side to him too.
'He's a posh southerner, for God's sake!'
Oh come on, he can't help that.
'I'm not his type.'
He just invited you to his tent.
Blast.

Breakfast the next morning was a little odd. Guy and I didn't say anything to anyone but everyone knew we'd shared a tent. No-one commented. They didn't know whether this was a drunken crash in a mate's tent, never to be repeated, or something more. Neither did I. Did Guy? No idea.
Anyway, I had a trip to run, so we packed up and got on the road as if nothing had happened.

CHAPTER TEN
Song, dance, laughter & tears

When you're young you inevitably accept a lot of words without explanation, and so you often make your own not-very-educated guess as to what something might mean. I knew the term 'whirling dervish' as something my nana would call my sister, Sam, and me on especially boisterous days.

'Would you *please* keep still for two minutes, girls. You're like whirling dervishes. You're making my head spin. Sit down for a bit!'

I was sure a dervish was a small, brown hairy creature something akin to the Loony Tunes character called the Tasmanian Devil, but with fewer teeth. I like to think that the founder of the real whirling dervishes, a thirteenth-century Persian poet and Sufi mystic called Rumi, would have had a giggle at this. After all, this was a man who recommended song, dance and laughter as the best ways of getting closer to God.

We were in the town of Konya in south-central Turkey and this is where Rumi lived much of his life and where he died. Before my first visit to Konya, I'd never heard of Rumi or his poetry, though by then I *had* heard of the whirling dervishes and now knew them to be part of the Sufi order of Islamic mysticism rather than cartoon characters. I also knew that they did indeed whirl, but it wasn't until I came to Konya that I discovered why. The whirling is a kind of physical meditation which aims to remove the ego and connect the dancer to God. I got the answer when we visited the Mevlana Museum so called because Rumi was also known as Mevlana, meaning 'our master'. This was the former lodge of the whirling dervishes and the place of Rumi's mausoleum and shrine. His mausoleum has a spectacular sixteen-lobed cylindrical tower topped with a conical roof, all covered with tiles of glazed turquoise faience. It's a thing of beauty and a fitting tribute to a man who taught that love and tolerance were the path to spiritual enlightenment.

You might not think that the words of a 750-year-old Muslim poet would have much appeal today, but you'd be wrong. The messages in his poetry have endured and they resonate today as much as they did in his time. Aphorisms attributed to Rumi offer motivation for us all to be the best people we can be and, as such, are ever-popular. One of my favourites was, *'It's your road and yours alone. Others may walk it with you, but no-one can walk it for you.'*

After a morning's drive and some sightseeing, the Rumi quote that was drawing me that day was *'Respond to every call that excites your spirit.'* I needed lunch! Yes, I know, very shallow, but Konya was also a place where you could get some seriously good food. I knew of a restaurant which made the best *etli ekmek*, a local dish which is a kind of pizza made of thin flatbread topped with spicy lamb mince, peppers, onions and tomatoes. I led the group there and luckily they could fit us in. Plate after plate of *etli ekmek* made its way to our tables and then a dish of roast lamb came too.

'Free for you. It's speciality here. Enjoy!' said the waiter.

Roast lamb is delicious at the best of times. This was better than the best of times. The lamb came out of a domed brick kiln-like oven and apparently it had been cooking for about seven hours. It was the most succulent, melt-in-the-mouth, tastiest lamb I'd had in my life. I looked across the table at Guy. His face said it all; he was in lamb heaven and he gave me a big smile. It was the first time I'd looked at him properly that day since I was unsure what to make of the night before and I was determined to keep things professional and not let on to the group that anything had happened. I smiled back. At that point, I felt sure that whatever happened next, and even if nothing happened next, we could continue enjoying each other's company and having fun for the rest of the trip. It was a happy meal, but it was also unexpectedly tinged with sadness — the end of this adventure was all too close. We had just two weeks left before we reached the UK.

It's surprising what you can pack into two weeks if you put your mind to it, and our friends were very serious about seeing as much of Turkey as they could. However, we were still a day behind schedule due to the accident in Egypt so something would have to give. Guy and I discussed it and agreed that if we did a full day's drive through Yugoslavia, we could have our full time in Turkey without missing our ferry from Belgium back to England.

'But it will mean about twenty-four hours driving almost non-stop except for breaks for food and the loo,' I told them all. 'Guy and I are willing to share the driving and do it, but it will be quite hard on you guys too. What do you reckon?'

They were all up for it, so we continued with the itinerary as it was meant to be in Turkey: the beautiful beaches of Olu Deniz and Fethiye, the hot springs and cotton castles of Pamukkale, the incredible remains of the Greco-Roman city of Ephesus, the First World War battlefields of Gallipoli, and finally, the fabulous city of Istanbul. Straddling Europe and Asia, Turkey has such a rich history that you more or less trip over sites of significant historical interest everywhere you go, its landmass is so varied that you're never short of fascinating or beautiful sights, and its people so diverse that it is a cultural treasure for the curious. For ten days more, we revelled in all things Turkish.

Having left Konya, we camped overnight near Isparta before heading down to the coast. In the morning we took time for a tour of the town's famous rose gardens. Isparta has been growing roses on an industrial scale for over a century and is the main global supplier of rose oil which is used for medicine, cosmetics and, far more importantly if you ask me, Turkish Delight. We'd missed the June harvest but there were plenty of blooms to enjoy and we walked around drinking in the heavenly perfume of both roses and lavender. The garden guide, Ahmet, knew a little German and some rudimentary English, so between his mediocre English and my unpractised German, we thought we'd got the gist of most things. At the end of the tour, he invited us all to a wedding celebration party in a nearby village.

'Come and eat. Very welcome,' he said. 'Big food, music and party.'

Spontaneity often brings rewards in travel so we accepted his kind invitation. In a village on the edge of town, a large garden was full of guests. Ahmet ushered us into a tent where delicious smells emanated from vast pans and cauldrons. We'd come bearing gifts of local wine and soon we were offered seats at a table.

'Please. Eat. Drink,' said Ahmet, and we willingly obliged. Plates of food began to arrive. Apparently about a thousand people would drift in and out during the day. This was truly mass catering.

We couldn't see the happy couple and after about half an hour I asked Ahmet if they would be coming soon.

'Who?'

'The newly weds. Die verheiratete leute. The married people.' He looked confused, then laughed.

'Come.' He pointed to me and Guy and we followed him into the nearby house. He led us upstairs. This was becoming rather odd.

'Wait,' he said, leaving us outside a door. He went in, then returned a few moments later.

'Come.'

It was a large bedroom with two single beds. There were a few people in the room, all standing, and sitting up in the beds were two young boys wearing bright red jackets. Matching red hats were on the bedside table, tall hats with feathered plumes at the front. A middle-aged man came over to us, welcoming us. Though confused as to who we were, he seemed pleased to see us and pointed proudly at the boys.

'These are his sons,' said Ahmet.

And then it dawned on us. It wasn't a wedding, it was a coming of age celebration. The boys had been recently circumcised. Unsurprisingly, they looked very uncomfortable and the younger one was crying silently. He took his hat from the table and put it under his sheets in a strategic position to stop any rubbing. Poor little chaps. We wished them well, said our goodbyes to the father, and went back downstairs.

You know that feeling of being so embarrassed that you just have to laugh? Well, keeping that laughter inside was not easy especially when we told our friends, who then also had to struggle to stop the guffawing that we were all dying to let out. We managed to remain polite, but oh, the effort!

I'd done this trip twice previously but this time it was different. On my first trip with Freddie, I'd been desperate to get everything right with the practicalities of the job — the driving, the cooking, the navigation, the mechanics — so whilst it had been a great trip, I hadn't had as much time as I'd have liked to fully explore and enjoy the places we visited. On my second trip, I was the leader and I had another fabulous group of people, but it was winter so a very different experience and also I felt I was fighting Ryan the whole way so it was mentally exhausting. This time, I was sure of my job, sure of where I was going and keen to share my knowledge of the amazing places on the trip, and now, I had a co-driver whose company I loved and who I could rely on to back me. It made everything so much easier and so much more enjoyable.

For most of us, after leaving the family home it's rare to spend almost every hour of every day with someone for weeks on end unless you're a couple or perhaps in the armed forces. There's no doubt that you get to know someone pretty well in such a scenario, especially when there are hard times as well as good times and you're working *and* playing together. But you still don't necessarily fall for them the way I was now falling for Guy. Perhaps it was because at the start of the trip I'd thought I wouldn't really get on with him and our relationship had grown slowly. My ambivalence towards him had quickly relaxed as I saw past the arrogance to someone who was certainly self-confident yet also quietly sensitive. Then the aftermath of the crash in Egypt had assured me that I could trust and rely on him in difficult situations, and with that and our shared love of exploring new places and cultures, friendship had quickly followed. I had neither expected nor looked for anything more. When things began to change, I was a muddle of happiness, confusion and reticence.

It's a holiday romance, I told myself, that's all. Just enjoy it for two weeks, then move on. He will.

But I knew I wasn't the holiday romance type. And what of Andy who I'd known since we'd got together at university and who I kept being drawn back to despite breaks in the relationship? There was no doubt I still loved and cared for him, but— but this was different. I almost knew Guy better after seven weeks together than I did Andy after seven on-and-off years.

I 'protected' myself from Guy by trying to keep things light and fun, but then something happened which rocked the shield over my heart. It happened at Gallipoli. Gallipoli is a peninsula in western Turkey and was the site of a First World War defeat of the allied forces including the Anzacs, the Australians and New Zealand forces against the Ottoman Empire in 1915/16, before the founding of the Republic of Turkey. All sides suffered heavy casualties here and there are many thousands of war graves in the area. It is always sobering to visit such a place but one of the reasons why travel is important is that when you see things rather than just read about them, places and events become more real, and in this case, more tragic. That is a good thing; we *should* remember. Humankind has become good at acknowledging and commemorating loss and tragedy through memorial sites such as these, but the pity is that we keep needing to add to them. We learn, but then we seem to forget, or a new situation compels someone in power to risk yet more lives. I realise that view will be far too simplistic for some, but when you're faced with row upon row of graves of young men, it's hard to see past the futility of their deaths.

Perhaps it was the sombre note of the day which led to Guy saying what he did, but at the campsite that night we stayed up late chatting in the cab after finishing writing up the route notes and updating accounts. The flippant, light-hearted Guy was nowhere to be seen as he turned to me and said, 'You know, you're seriously special.'

That wasn't fair. We didn't say things like that. I didn't know what to say. I looked at him, words not forming.

'It's all right,' he said, 'I understand about Andy, and I don't expect anything.'

I nodded, still dumb. Then someone coughed quite loudly in one of the tents. I was glad of the release from the moment, and we both laughed.

'It seems we have an audience!' he said. 'Shall we call it a day?'

Nothing more was said the following day, nor the next three days in Istanbul, nor all the rest of the journey to the ferry, in fact nothing else was said at all.

The whole group was still having great fun but I think we all had in mind that our adventure was nearly over. Leaving Turkey for Greece, we had one last blowout on the beach — a barbecue, lots of beers, and Pete and Guy singing and playing guitar until late — but then we stocked up the coolbox with water and softies, bought lots of snacks and food for an easy-to-cook meal, and headed for Yugoslavia. Our twenty-four-hour marathon catch-up drive began.

Guy and I drove two hours on and two hours off. After the first few stints, we each managed to sleep on our breaks. About ten hours into the drive we had an hour-long stop in a grotty truck park to make dinner. It was a relief for us all to get out and stretch, and for the noise of the truck and the road to stop for a while. We were all tired but we knew we still had a long way to go. No-one complained. For want of anywhere pleasant to walk, I decided to dance around the truck as a form of escape. Perhaps Rumi had been right when he said, *'In order to understand stillness, one must dance.'* In my yellow cotton frock, I twirled, jumped, skipped and generally pranced about like an idiot. It was a blessed release after hours of driving and sitting. At one point I noticed that everyone was looking at me as if I had lost my marbles, but they said nothing and I carried on in my own little world. We ate, then got back on the road. It was a very hard night, and one which I'd not like to repeat — I like my sleep — but we did it.

By the time we got on the ferry for the overnight crossing, we were all a bit sad it was at an end, but equally, we knew we'd made some good friendships and had a trip that was going to remain with us for a long time. I was partly happy to be heading home to see my mum, dad and sister, and to find out what was next on my personal overlanding adventure, but partly anxious and miserable that my time with Guy was nearly over.

Three weeks later, I was at Heathrow Airport. Guy and I had seen a lot of each other since we got back, and he'd volunteered to drive me down to catch my plane to Harare in Zimbabwe. I was going to meet up with Freddie again for a six-month journey back to the UK via West Africa. It was the perfect trip, the one I'd longed for for two years. I wanted to go but I would sorely miss my family and I didn't want to leave Guy. I knew this would be the end of our short relationship. He was heading off in a few days to drive from the UK to Kathmandu and then around India. Our paths would not be crossing for a long time, probably at least a year, if ever again.

We'd both studiously avoided saying goodbye up until then, but it was nearly time to part. Guy started to say something as we got closer to the departure gate.

'That day we drove for twenty-four hours, when you danced around the truck— '

I was desperately trying to choke back tears and confused as to why he would suddenly want to reminisce about that part of the trip. I wasn't going to be able to keep things together for much longer.

'Please go before I cry,' I said.

His face seemed to darken, but he nodded and then gave me an envelope.

'These are my *poste restante* dates. I've got yours. Maybe write to me?'

'I will,' I said, with a wobbly smile, and stuffed the letter in my bag.

'Cheers then,' he said, and turned and walked away. Just like that. Gone. No kiss. No 'I'll miss you.' Nothing. And why hadn't I said something? Too late. I watched. He didn't look back.

I was flying to Africa, the place I'd wanted to go since first starting this adventure. Tears poured down my cheeks.

PART THREE

AFRICA

CHAPTER ELEVEN
Red dust & river gods

'Hey, Amanda! Welcome to Africa!' Freddie gave me a big bear hug. 'You're going to love it here and it'll be great driving with you again.'

After fourteen hours of flying, and crying for far too long, I was in a state of exhaustion from lack of sleep. I'd left the UK having ended my relationship with Andy with a promise to remain friends, said tearful farewells to Mum, Dad and Sam, and parted from Guy, for good, I was convinced. I felt very alone. But I was in Africa, actual sub-Saharan Africa. This was a new start. I had to pull myself together. I would be a bloody fool to waste this opportunity.

It was late July 1990 and we had about ten days to get everything ready before the group joined us for the first leg of the trans-Africa trip, a five-week journey from Harare in Zimbabwe to Nairobi in Kenya. It was the trip I'd first set my heart on back in Cirencester when Sheena egged me on to call Dragoman. Thank God for friends who chivvy you into doing what's good for you. Most people were only joining us for this section but four of this group of eighteen would be staying with us for the full six months all the way back to the UK, along with eight more joining us in Nairobi. Freddie and I were both crossing our fingers for a great bunch of people. Six months is a long time.

My first few days in Africa were in the bustling city of Harare dealing with the usual whirl of preparations for the start of a new trip — mending tents, truck maintenance, sorting paperwork and money, and buying the bulk food staples such as rice, flour, pasta, tea, coffee, jam . . . all the usual dried and tinned foodstuffs which we could then supplement with fresh meat, fruit and veg from markets along the way. I'd been warned that shopping on this trip wasn't as easy as on the Egypt & Middle East journey, but at least we didn't have to find ice. This truck had the luxury of a fridge.

'Oh yes,' said Freddie, 'and not only a fridge but I've had a little addition made for Huwey.' Huwey was the truck's name since the number plate began with UWE.

'Ta dah!' Freddie unrolled a huge blue and white-striped awning which came out from the edge of the roof and was then held up with two long steel poles and guy ropes. 'What do you reckon?'

'I reckon we'll look like a mobile butcher's shop,' I said, laughing. 'But yes, I like it!'

Freddie looked pleased. 'It'll be great for lunch stops. You know, either as a sun shade or if it's raining.'

Freddie was never happier than when tinkering or mending. Sitting still wasn't his thing, he always had to be doing — something, anything — but then, at the end of each day, it was as if his batteries died.

The first few days of any group adventure is a mix of excitement and trepidation — for the leaders as well as the passengers. Everyone tends to make a really big effort to be as sociable and pleasant as possible as they slowly work out who they get on with, where closer friendships might be made, who are the good cooks or the work-shirkers, who has a sense of humour and who doesn't. For many this was easy and fun but this was the bit I continued to find daunting. Despite my experiences over the last couple of years with Dragoman, I still wasn't confident in social situations with unknown people. I was usually fine once I'd got the measure of someone, but until then . . . well, I found it quite stressful and tiring. Because of this, I needed to escape when I could — a bit tricky when you're the co-driver partly responsible for ensuring a truck full of people were having a good time.

Driving out of Harare, we were very soon into the Africa I'd been desperate to see. The tarmac quickly gave way to gravel or baked mud roads running like scars through the parched landscape. Being August, it was both winter and the dry season. Stupidly, I hadn't expected the cold to be quite so cold here. Mornings and evenings could easily drop to freezing. One of my first purchases was a cosy blanket as my cheap sleeping bag was now more tea towel than duvet.

On our second day, we stopped for lunch on the side of a mud road well away from any huts or villages. Huwey attracted children like moths to a flame, perhaps because we were a white truck with an orange stripe and an orange tarpaulin covering the kit we stored on the roof. We didn't exactly blend in.

'Freddie, I'm going to skip lunch and walk ahead if that's all right with you. I just want a bit of time to myself.'

'Yeah, no worries. I'll save you a sandwich. Don't get lost.'

Not much chance of that. This road offered no deviation from its purpose of reaching Binga on the shores of Lake Kariba. I started walking away from the truck and my new companions. At first, I strode out with the determined steps of someone going on an exercise walk, but after about five minutes, with the truck almost out of sight around a slight bend and dip, I started to relax, slow down and looked around.

Beneath the kingfisher blue sky, lemon yellow, ochre and nut brown leaves clung to hibernating mopane trees and the sun illuminated the underlying dried grasses to give a golden haze to the landscape. The earth was red, but that was far too common a word for this colour. This red was vibrant and full of life even though it was winter. It was the red of a freshly-chopped alder tree that seems to bleed once it's cut — one last explosion of colour before it returns to the earth. And as I walked, the African soil began to claim me. The fine alder-blood dust rose to coat my bare feet and legs and then, drifting higher, the smell enveloped me. Baked cinnamon with a touch of hot chocolate and a pinch of rosemary. I walked as if all alone in the world and, despite still knowing very little about Zimbabwe and Africa in general, I felt at one with my surroundings and happy in this land so untouched by humans. I instinctively knew I was going to be happy here.

'Baaap!' said Huwey, as Freddie drove up behind me. That was the end of my 'me time' reverie and I climbed back into the passenger seat of the cab. As we set off, Nicky came up to the cab proffering a ham sandwich but I didn't feel like eating.

'Okay,' she said, turning round to the group with a wicked smile, 'anyone want Amanda's ham sandwich? Come on girls, you're not going to get much meat on this trip, so you might as well dig in!'

Ah yes, Nicky was going to be good fun.

And fun was definitely the order of the day for the five days we had in the town of Victoria Falls.

The world-famous falls are known locally as *Mosi-oa-Tunya* meaning 'The Smoke that Thunders.' Thank heavens this beautifully descriptive name wasn't lost to rampant colonialism but remained as a poetic connection between language and landscape. And, if you'll excuse a cliché, the falls really are poetry in motion. A wide curtain of water hurls itself into the deep chasm that's been chiselled out of the basalt rock over millennia. Water becomes the fire from which the smoke rises to be seen for miles around on this otherwise flat plateau. The sun tints these billowing clouds with pinks and oranges as the evening draws in, and when the moon is full, rainbows dance above the thunder, just out of reach of the raging waters.

There was so much to do here: the 'Flight of the Angels' over the falls, whitewater rafting, horse riding, and bungee-jumping off the bridge between Zambia and Zimbabwe. But the first thing Freddie arranged for the group was the 'booze' cruise — a gorgeous sunset cruise on the Zambezi River (above the falls), with a free bar. It sounded dangerous, and indeed so it turned out to be for many. But it was also the event which made everyone gel together as any remaining pretences were washed away with copious Castle lagers. Friendships were consolidated that night and from then on I noticed everyone pulling together and looking out for each other in a way that was more second nature than it had been. I think we were all glad of that when, two days later, we headed off in the morning to clamber down the ravine into Batoka Gorge just past the foot of Victoria Falls near the so-called Boiling Pot. We had life jackets and helmets and we'd each been given an oar. Whitewater rafting anyone?

I'm not hugely keen on putting my face under water, and a fear of drowning doesn't sit altogether comfortably with the idea of rafting one of the world's most difficult and notorious stretches of river, especially in low-water season.

'Nyaminyami is the Zambezi river god,' said one of our rafting guides. 'At this time of year, he can be a malevolent scumbag.'

I didn't like the sound of that at all but I'd come for an

adventure and I could hardly be the one to pike out. I gritted my teeth, taped my glasses to my head with a secure and very attractive contraption of duct tape, and headed with the group to our two awaiting rafts.

The Zambezi zig-zags away from Victoria Falls as if trying to evade a predator that's hot on its heels. Raptors love the precipitous cliffs of the gorge, and pied kingfishers can be seen fishing in the stretches of deceptively calm water, but mostly, the local wildlife knows better. This is the realm of rafters and kayakers.

'Don't worry about the crocodiles if you see one,' said the guide. 'They're not usually big enough to prey on humans.'

Now why couldn't he have left out the word 'usually'?

The International Scale of River Difficulty classes whitewater river rapids from grade I, which is easy, to grade VI which is deemed to be 'extraordinarily difficult and guaranteed to put rafters in constant and imminent danger of death'. The Zambezi is a grade V river, so it's only 'extremely difficult'. Well, that's all right then, given that we're all novices apart from Freddie. And just how are you supposed to hang on for dear life with a paddle in your hands? I didn't like the answer from our guide, Vincent, a super-enthusiastic young Zimbabwean who had not one ounce of fat covering the wiry muscles of his arms or the well-defined six-pack underneath his life jacket.

'You must keep hold of your paddle at all times. When I say "high-side right front", anyone in the front rushes to the front right side of the raft to weigh us down so we don't flip. Okay? Likewise "high-side left" and so on. Got it? And if I say "Paddle right", the rafters on the right paddle like mad, or "Get down", well, I guess that's pretty obvious.'

In fact, most of the instructions were pretty obvious but that didn't stop the whole idea being as scary as hell. I just wanted a bloody great bar to cling onto like on a fairground ride but all you could do was wedge your feet as well as you could into the rubber raft as you sat on the edge (the edge, for God's sake!). There was a rope around the raft, but it was quite loose and seemed rather pointless.

'And if you get flipped out or we flip totally—' (You have got to be joking!) '—then you grab onto the rope if you can. If you can't, just lay on your back, cross your arms and go feet first downriver. I promise we'll pull you out.'

The morning did not begin gently. Starting at Rapid 1, you're straight into a grade IV rapid. My heart hammered in my chest as we closed in on the raging waters. Vincent was sitting on a metal frame in the middle of the large raft and had long oars to manoeuvre us. He used the eight of us to fine-tune our approach and, hopefully, keep us upright.

Oh my good God, let me out, let me out, let me—

'Paddle right, paddle right!' Vincent screamed over the roar of the furious water. I did as I was ordered. There was no way out of this now. Then, a few seconds later, 'Stop!'

'High-side front. Now!'

I threw myself to the front of the raft and was immediately squashed into the rubber as Freddie landed on top of me to add his solid weight to the bow. We were utterly drenched and drinking far too much Zambezi as the river god tried to flip us over from front to back.

'Paddle left,' yelled Vincent.

That was me. We righted ourselves and I started paddling through the frantic white waves, feeling the rage of Nyaminyami under the thin rubber beneath my feet. We were nearly through but still being buffeted.

91

'Swimmer!' someone shouted from the back. The great 'Slambezi' had claimed its first victim. Who was it? I looked into the water and saw the little Irish nurse, Anita, bobbing up and down through the last and thankfully calmer section of the rapid. Vincent was with her in seconds and we hauled her back in the raft as the river transformed itself into a benign force of nature that wouldn't dream of upsetting anyone. Anita was laughing hysterically. Wait, we were *all* laughing hysterically. We hadn't drowned, we were all in one piece, and the adrenalin surge was incredible. After that first rapid, I didn't have time to panic or be frightened at all, and the constant exhilaration was like nothing I'd ever experienced. We steamed through *Morning Glory* (grade IV), screamed through *Stairway to Heaven* (grade V), and chilled through the *Devil's Toilet Bowl* (a mere grade III). The only rapid we didn't tackle, despite feeling quite gung-ho by then, was rapid number nine known as *Commercial Suicide* (grade VI), which we portaged around, carrying the raft over the slippery, rocky riverbank before continuing downriver.

At the end of a thrilling morning, we had to climb out of the gorge carrying all our kit. It was a real struggle for some of the group as exhaustion began to take over from euphoria. As I trekked upwards, noticing a rare Taita falcon soaring overhead, it dawned on me not only how fit I'd become over the last couple of years but what an incredible life I'd accidentally chosen for myself. Look at me, the girl who swims like a seahorse because she doesn't like getting her face wet has just rafted on the Zambezi River in Zimbabwe!

Nature, or perhaps Nyaminyami, had shared some of her strength and confidence with me and I think that was the first time in my life I felt a little bit powerful.

CHAPTER TWELVE
28,000 Miles. One Lion

[To Await Arrival, Poste Restante, Esfahan, Iran]

Victoria Falls, 19th August 1990
Dear Guy,
Well, this news probably won't surprise you at all, but I'm in love. In love with Africa! It's like a very hot Autumn here during the day. The colours are wonderful, the smells are intoxicating and the heat is delicious · · · until nightfall when it's freezing.
I have all these sudden urges to write poetry or paint about what I'm seeing, so I bought a drum (!) and I'm trying to learn how to sketch with charcoal and pastels. I'm also finding myself singing and smiling a bit too much. People are going to start thinking I'm happy. I feel unconstrained. I can breathe. And can you believe I actually went whitewater rafting? What a fantastic day that was!
I'm also becoming a shit-hot corrugated road driver. It's excellent fun, isn't it? Bombing along at 60kph getting rattled to death and then seeing a bloody great ditch just in front of you! I'm amazed we've still got whole springs. Huwey is the best truck, though not the fastest

milk-cart on the road, especially as we reckon we're carrying about 14 tons at the moment with all the stuff we've got with us to get us home.

We have a great group of people, four going all the way including a 56-year-old man called John who seems great. Freddie is a great bloke, it's good to be back with him. I really like him, but he's a difficult man to share things with, and as you know I enjoy things so much more if I share with someone I like. With you it was easy. Anyway, I'd like you to know that even if you're happily enrapt with someone else now, this girl misses your company.

Hugs and kisses, Amanda xx

Up until Victoria Falls, I hadn't decided how I was going to write to Guy or even *if* I was going to write to him. But the rafting had given my confidence and positivity a shot in the arm, and I made up my mind that I didn't want to lose touch with this man who'd touched my heart probably more than he realised. I kept it light and short, told the truth in terms of how I missed him, but didn't let on the whole truth of how I thought about him every day, wondered constantly where and how he was, and desperately wanted him with me. With luck he'd get this letter by early September and maybe I'd get a letter from him in Nairobi which was my only post date on this section of the trip.

Trying to stay in contact with anyone if you were on the road in 1990 was a bit of a mission. Mobile phones were rare and for the super-rich, the Internet was only just starting, and a phone call home cost £1 per minute (a staggering price at the time) so was unaffordable except for emergencies. We sent the occasional fax or telex to Dragoman, but letters were our main means of communication with friends and family so visits to the poste restante to pick up post were a highlight on any long trip. The news would invariably be old by the time you read it, but at least it was contact.

By the time we reached Zambia, I was still searching for my first lion. Zimbabwe had been a total disappointment on that score so I was crossing my fingers for Zambia.

It felt much edgier here than in Zimbabwe. I discovered that there had been an attempted coup just seven weeks earlier on 1st July, so president Kenneth Kaunda and his followers were rather jittery. KK had been in power for twenty-six years, since the country gained independence from Britain in 1964, but he was seen as being increasingly inept, particularly in regards to the dreadful food shortages in recent times. Very few tourists came to Zambia as there was little decent infrastructure and far too much political instability. In Zimbabwe we passed smiling faces everywhere and children waved like mad things as they ran alongside the truck, but in Zambia we'd been met a few times with signs of a finger being drawn across the neck. Adrian was nearly arrested at one point just for walking through a village with a camera over his shoulder. It made for an occasionally tense journey north and whenever we stopped in towns or villages we took turns to guard the truck in groups of four. We always kept things friendly with anyone who came up to speak with us, but we certainly felt that leaving the truck alone, even locked, wasn't a great idea.

Eventually, though, leaving villages behind and crossing the bridge over the Luangwa River, we were welcomed into the wild realm of South Luangwa by grunting hippos, a procession of helmeted guinea fowl and the iridescent flash of a lilac-breasted roller.

The pristine wilderness of South Luangwa National Park is beautiful, truly beautiful. In summer, twisty brown tributaries run through lush grasslands and past plentiful miombo and mopane forests until they swell the meandering Luangwa River, the life-sustaining saviour of this ancient, mineral-rich Rift Valley. But this was winter, when the unforgiving sun sucks every last drop of moisture from the land and plants, and the river is a trickle of its summer self. Majestic mahoganies, bizarre sausage trees and magical groves of ebony thrive partly by hugging the riverbanks, but winter is mostly a desperate struggle for survival for both flora and fauna. And yet, somehow, wildlife does find a way to live here. Not without cost, of course — death is an all too real part of life here — but this is nature and no-one ever said nature was kind. What she does tend to be, however, is balanced; at least until we humans start sticking our oar in. In South Luangwa in 1990, mankind had thankfully not yet decided to rape this land of its resources, other than the very sad poaching of its wildlife, so it was remarkably and stunningly preserved. We were in an African Eden. Thousands of hippos squabbled and jostled for space in the larger pools of the river, zebras dazzled dustily, giraffes towered above young apple leaf trees, baboons trooped about looking for honey and trouble, lions—

'Over there, on the right at about two o'clock, under that bush,' shouted John.

He was right. Freddie stopped the truck. The sleeping lion had melted into the sandy earth, but he deigned to raise his handsome head and acknowledge our presence. He was a young male and his beautiful golden eyes were circumscribed with dark fur making it look like he'd assiduously applied his eyeliner that morning. An old scar ran just under his left eye to his whiskers, and his dusky pink nose had dark freckles and a notch out of the left side. We were very close and yet he seemed totally disinterested in this truck full of admiring humans. He blinked slowly, took a leisurely look around, then, obviously deciding there was nothing worth getting up for, laid his magnificent head back on his huge paws and closed his eyes.

Oh, be still my beating heart! I'd actually seen my first lion. I wanted to do all the things I knew I couldn't and shouldn't: get even closer, rush out and hug him, or wake him up so he'd move or at least look at us again. I yearned for a stronger connection. My quest to see a wild lion had begun over two years ago and I'd driven 28,000 miles (more than the equatorial circumference of the Earth) to find him. Was it worth it? Hell, yes! Here was my Aslan in his very own Narnia . . . and I was here too. I hoped Freddie and the group couldn't see the child within me screaming and jumping up and down with barely contained delight, but they certainly saw the huge grin on my face. It seemed a lifetime since that mugging in a snowy park in Leeds where I promised myself I would be more lion and less mouse. My inner mouse had been shown the door, but the gap it left had not yet been filled with the essence of lion. I decided that the memory of this handsome chap would be my talisman as I continued my search.

I would have happily stayed all day to see what this king of beasts might do, though knowing domestic cats as I did, I guessed that might not be very much in the daytime heat. Anyway, understandably, I doubted the rest of the group would be keen on such a limited safari.

As we carried on with our game drive, I didn't think anything else would come close to seeing the lion. But I was wrong. At the gloopy remnants of a nearby waterhole, we came across a family of five elephants including a baby. The baby had got right into the waterhole and was now struggling to extricate himself. He wasn't seriously stuck, he was just too young to have much control over his limbs or his floppy little trunk. Again and again, he ended up on his back, legs flailing comically until mum and the aunties decided to put a stop to his antics and joined forces to coax and help him out of the sticky mud bath. They worked together, sharing their strength and gentleness. Wrinkly grey legs pushed and supported, and four dexterous trunks nudged and held the little body allowing him to clamber his way out. It was at once funny and touching. Upright and free, the baby immediately set off at a racing trot with his trunk pointing straight out in front of him towards a laughing dove he'd spotted. I may not have actually heard or seen the adult elephants tutting and rolling their eyes whilst smiling fondly, but I know they did.

'How can anyone look at such a magnificent, intelligent animal and want to kill it?' I said, mostly to myself. The local guide we'd employed for the day, Daniel, was sitting on the black box between me and Freddie, and he turned to me.

'You know, it is hard to live here. I was lucky, I got an education and I have work, but many people in the valley, they do not. No-one here really wants to kill an animal except for food. If they are struggling, they will maybe take an impala or a warthog some time to feed their family. Poaching is not good and it is illegal here, but if your children are hungry, what do you do?'

'Yes, I can see the dilemma,' I said. And I did. It's easy to take the moral high ground with a full belly. 'But what about killing elephants for their tusks? That's not subsistence poaching. That's just about ivory and money. It's about killing for greed, surely?'

'It's bad,' he said, nodding. 'I think local people don't do this. This is bad people from outside of the valley.'

Being a local boy, I guessed it would have been hard for him to accept that people in his community were poaching elephants for their ivory, so I could understand him blaming it on outsiders. I found it hard to believe that locals had nothing to do with any poaching going on in their patch, but now was not the time for such a discussion. We had just one full day to enjoy this wondrous park.

As safari novices, I'm afraid to say that most of us, including me, had very little interest in the birds that Daniel skilfully pointed out to us. We wanted to see more elephants, more big cats, zebras, giraffes . . . all the big, iconic mammals of the African bush. However, my indifference to birds was soon shaken.

'There's a weird kind of cloud over there, near the ground,' said Freddie, pointing, and straining to see what he was looking at.

The cloud was moving. It was like a piece of tumbleweed but huge and much more fluid, sometimes rising a little, speeding up, slowing down. It was heading towards us.

'Queleas,' said Daniel, 'also called red-billed weaver birds. There are so many they're a pest, but they are fascinating. Listen, here they come.'

As the murmuration got even closer, we heard thousands of tiny wings agitate the hot dry air in a cacophony of chitter-chatter. One little red-billed weaver bird might have been boring to me; tens of thousands were anything but. I imagined this would be similar to what a plague of locusts would look like and their effect on farmers' crops would no doubt be similarly devastating, but I couldn't help being utterly transfixed and awed by these feisty creatures. This behaviour was all about safety in numbers. When birds of prey saw one huge writhing entity, they were less likely to attack, and if they did, the odds of each individual weaver bird surviving were far greater within the huge flock. Clever little queleas.

My love of nature started as a love of flowers when I won a junior school wild flower competition. I always loved immersing myself in the great outdoors around our house in Durham's rural hills. I would walk our dogs for miles and horse ride across wind-battered expanses of heather and bilberry-covered fells. My love of animals was initially limited to domestic pets or farm animals and I dreamed of becoming a vet like James Herriot or perhaps a farmer. I was disabused of both of these ideas by the time I was sixteen — one thanks to that physics teacher and the other because, not being from a farming family, I didn't think farming was open to me. It never dawned on me that there were other avenues I could have considered to work with animals. Careers advisers at that time were hugely lacking in imagination, as, it seemed, was I.

Nevertheless, here I was, in the middle of Africa, surrounded by animals, and this was part of my job! Life on Earth really was as mesmerising as David Attenborough said it was. Lions might have drawn me to this continent, and I would always have a very soft spot for big cats, but this safari in Zambia pushed the doors of my heart wide-open to the bigger picture of Nature. I learned two important things that day: that Africa would always be very special to me, and that I wanted to know and see much more of the world's wildlife and natural environments. I felt energised, excited and supremely happy, but I had so many questions. Of course, I was on a journey to explore much more of Africa than just its national parks but I promised myself that, one day, I would find a way to return. I would come back with far fewer people, I would stay longer, I would learn about the grasses, trees, flowers, animals and, yes, even the birds, and I would drink long and deep of the joy and freedom of being in the wild.

CHAPTER THIRTEEN
Tyrants and spice

I knew almost nothing about our next destination, Malawi, apart from it being one of Africa's poorest countries and that, weirdly, Lonely Planet's travel guide *Africa on a Shoestring* was banned here. I also remembered Guy telling me that when he tried to enter the country on his own trip in 1983, he had hair almost down to his waist and he was told that he wouldn't be allowed in unless he cut it off above the collar because he was a bloody hippy. He was gutted but he hacked at his locks with the pair of blunt scissors he was offered. I quickly discovered that this and the country's many other rules, such as women not being allowed to wear trousers, came from His Excellency the Life President of the Republic of Malawi, Ngwazi Dr. Hastings Kamuzu Banda. Until he was ousted in 1994, the country was ruled with the doctor's gloved fist, and surgical precision when it came to looking for dissenters. You were either for him or against him, and you definitely didn't want to be against this highly educated tyrant since he had a network of informers and the outcome for such a stance was generally unpleasant or deadly. He once said that if anyone opposed him they would be 'food for crocodiles'. Such a healer.

Dr Banda would probably have been apoplectic if he'd seen our antics at the beach at Cape Maclear on Lake Malawi. Malawi is a land-locked country but about a third of its territory is covered by Lake Malawi which is roughly 365 miles long and fifty-two miles wide, earning it the nickname the 'calendar lake'. It is such a vast body of water that, other than the fact that it is fresh water and not tidal, it seems very much like a sea. And it has beautiful beaches, one of which is at Cape Maclear at the southern end of the lake. We had two full days here. Free time to relax and let our hair down. Well, not the men, obviously.

I'd been quite ill with a stomach upset and hellish headaches for the last week. Evelyn and Anita, our Australian and Irish nurses, reckoned I had a recurrence of giardia, a parasitic infection I'd first contracted in Egypt. Our arrival at the lake happily coincided with me feeling much better, though, so I could properly enjoy an easy couple of days.

Sometimes you need to reset yourself by doing very little of consequence, and this chilled couple of days gave me a pause and time to recognise that I was feeling very comfortable with this friendly group of people. During the day, I swam, drank Earl Grey tea, I wrote my diary and I sketched. Anita taught me how to make a friendship bracelet and we shopped at nearby stalls. I commissioned a foot-long straw-woven version of Huwey that was delivered to me on our second day. I was blown away by the skill needed to make this model, which came complete with a realistically forward-tilting cab and opening doors. I also fell in love with a Malawi chair — thank goodness for our roof storage — that had an impressively-carved back with an elephant at the top, three crowned cranes in the middle, and a roaring lion at the base just above the plain seat. My last major purchase was a wooden board game of Bau which I then tried to learn from the locals on the beach, much to their amusement.

There was always work to be done on the truck, of course, so I also spent time happily pottering — tightening bolts, changing filters, greasing, painting, cleaning — until Dave, Mark and Adrian decided I was too grubby to be seen with the rest of the group for dinner and threw me in the lake. Freddie was in happy mode too. He spent time replacing the broken cowl of our air intake with a small aluminium saucepan he'd painted black whilst prancing about in a frilly pink tutu. I told you Dr Banda wouldn't like it. A local boy called Goodrick helped us spit roast a goat, we had a few bottles of Mateus Rose wine (oh, we knew how to live), and we danced on the beach at night to tapes of Johnny Clegg & Juluka, and the addictive tunes of Zairois musician Kanda Bongo Man, plus Abba, Queen, Toto and Crowded House. Music tastes on the truck were eclectic. Life was good and we all agreed that Malawi, known as the 'warm heart of Africa' (no thanks to Dr Banda) was wonderful, at least for visitors if not for all its citizens.

Leaving the southern beaches two days later, we headed for Tanzania driving north up the western shore of the lake. Malawi might not have been a rainbow nation in terms of its politics but its landscapes and its people sang with colour. Everywhere you looked were lake views sparkling with turquoise and silver or forested hills in palettes of blues, greens, oranges and purples. Women wore long dresses in rich reds, juicy limes and clashing pinks, and shop owners in wooden shacks declared their wares through boldly painted murals with glorious slogans such as 'God is my Barber'.

It was slow but easy driving here so, whenever I got the chance, I sat in what we called the dog box. When you opened the roof hatches above the back seats, there were four extra seats where you were almost sitting on the truck roof. Up there, you could feel the sun on your back and the wind in your hair. Wherever we travelled, it was normal to see local people grabbing lifts on top of massively overladen lorries, so you often found yourself saying hi to groups of precariously balanced hitchhikers with a basket of hens on their knee, or coming eye to eye with a truck-surfing goat. This was my place for daydreaming. Inevitably, my thoughts drifted to Guy. Did he get my letter? Would there be one from him in Nairobi? I could hear him singing, *'Little darling, I feel that ice is slowly —'*

'Branch!' yelled a voice beneath me.

I ducked.

Dar es Salaam seemed huge after the many days we'd spent in rural areas or tiny villages, but we were just there to park up Huwey and escape to the spice islands of Zanzibar. I didn't dare ask what the group thought when they saw the boat, but I nearly decided against the trip when I saw the state of it. We had to wade out to this wreck of a tub and, once on board and on our way, the diesel fumes nearly knocked us sideways if the waves didn't. *Seaworthy* was not the word for this craft. *Seasick* was definitely the word for me. It was the most hideous boat journey I've ever undertaken and even before we landed I was dreading the return trip. By the age of twenty-six, my easy-to-read, glass face had learned how to perfect a gruesome shade of grey to tell the world if I was ever ill. On this occasion, the fact that I threw up all the contents of my stomach throughout the excruciating four-hour trip probably trumped the grey skin thing.

Arriving at Stone Town, the island's capital, I wasn't faced with the lush tropical idyll I'd expected. The place looked even greyer than I felt. The rambling muddle of once-white and once-grand buildings looked as if they'd caught an infection of black mould and were slowly decaying. Zanzibar had come under the rule of the Sultanate of Oman in the seventeenth century. A ruling Arab elite had been in power from then until it became a British Protectorate in 1890. Then, in 1964, a people's revolution eventually led to the islands becoming part of Tanzania. Without the wealth of the sultans, Stone Town's infrastructure began to crumble. The Sultan's Palace on the waterfront was empty and forlorn, and the House of Wonders, so called because it was the first building in Zanzibar to have electricity and a lift, had obviously suffered from many years of neglect. Since tourism had not yet been recognised as the money-spinner it would become, visitors were mainly backpackers and overlanders — and we didn't have much spending power. The best hotel in town was a disappointment of concrete with chairs that seemed to be made of wooden pallets, but sitting on their verandah at sunset with a cold beer or a G&T in hand and overlooking the Indian Ocean, well, we felt pretty rich. Perhaps not up to the standards of the islands' old sultans and their aristocrats but that was fine by us; their riches were steeped in blood. The blood of elephants and slaves.

During the eighteenth and nineteenth centuries, hundreds of thousands of brutalised and starving men, women and children were forced onto overcrowded dhows sailing from various parts of mainland East Africa to the Zanzibar archipelago. If they died during the trip, they were thrown overboard. If they didn't, they were doomed to the living nightmare of being sold at one of Zanzibar's many appalling slave markets, the largest and cruelest being in the middle of Stone Town.

From a distance, Zanzibar probably always looked like a stunningly beautiful place. David Livingstone liked it well enough to make it his base for many of his Victorian-era expeditions. But scratch the surface and, for at least two centuries, there was almost no kindness or true beauty to be found on this island. All was tainted. Until slavery was abolished here in 1897, this was an island of greed and brutality, pain and suffering. Zanzibar's leaders and magnates not only *sold* slaves but they used and abused them in their many thousands to farm expensive spices, especially cloves.

Ivory was key to the slave trade, as slaves were needed to carry the heavy tusks overland from the African interior. An average slave was worth far less to the traders than ivory. Literally millions of elephants were slaughtered for their tusks over these dreadful years, causing the African elephant population to drop from an estimated twenty-five million in 1600 to around ten million by the early 1900s.

In place of the slave market in Stone Town there was a large church, with the altar marking the spot where the horrific whipping post once stood; a place where slaves were viciously beaten to help set their value — the more pain they could withstand, the higher their price. Some might argue that it was a good thing that traces of the hideous slave trade were few and far between, but I found the lack of an appropriate acknowledgement rather odd.

Many years later, I returned to Stone Town and I was moved to see a very fitting though painful slave memorial sculpture. Made in 1998 by Clara Sornas, this haunting outdoor memorial successfully shows the trauma and total lack of hope in the faces of five slaves in a deep pit. Each slave wears a rusty iron collar attached to iron chains which bind them all together. These are original iron artefacts. There is also now a nearby Slave Trade

Heritage Centre where you can even visit a couple of the original underground cells where slaves were imprisoned in horrific conditions prior to being sold. They made me feel sick.

I walked through the narrow dusty streets of Stone Town and despite the rather dreary look of the place, I soon started to warm to it. Its Arabic ambience reminded me of many of the places I'd come to know and love in the Middle East. It was like being in a souk but without the same hustle and bustle and abundance of goods for sale. With familiarity came a relaxed contentment and a gentle awareness that I was beginning to see the world in context, to make connections . . . to feel like I belonged. Belonging brings a sense of freedom because you're no longer desperate to impress. If you belong, you've been accepted. If someone else has accepted you, you can give yourself the kindness of accepting yourself. But first you have to find yourself, your true self, warts and all.

Nadia and I came across an old photography studio. From the outside, Capital Art Studio was a curious, dingy little time-warp of a place but we were drawn in by the stunning black and white photos of old Zanzibar. When we entered, an Indian man with a beaming smile welcomed us.

'My father took most of these photographs,' explained Rohit Oza, looking fondly around at the many images on the walls of the small studio. 'After he came here from Gujarat, he started this shop in 1930 and he became photographer to Sultan Khalifa.'

We both bought a few beautifully reproduced prints of Zanzibar, my favourite being of a man in a white collared shirt and white flannel trousers cycling through the narrow streets and looking not unlike Sebastian Flyte in *Brideshead Revisited*. We also agreed to have our photograph taken with one of the old cameras, returning a short time later to collect it.

We opened the thin card envelope which held the image, and there we were. Nadia, looking her gorgeous self: big eyes, wavy brown hair and a wide friendly smile. And me. I saw me. I hadn't seen myself for a while, not really. I've never liked having my photograph taken as I didn't tend to like what I saw: a girl with crooked teeth and small eyes and a hairstyle that was neither one thing nor another. I wasn't keen on Rohit's image of me either, but I had to admit to seeing . . . well, a slightly different me. My eyes were different. The young woman looking at me had a twinkle. I couldn't exactly say that it was self-assurance but there was certainly less meekness, much more curiosity and a healthy dose of joie de vivre. It looked like my face was tagging along on this journey of mine and making some notes of its own.

After a night in Stone Town, we headed for the east coast. Here, at last, was the island I thought I was coming to see. You know the image we all have in our minds of the perfect tropical beach: palm trees and pink bougainvillea blossoms lining fine white sand beaches lapped by turquoise blue waters? This was it. Heaven. There were hardly any other tourists, and the choice of hotels . . . actually, there wasn't really a choice and we had to split up and stay in two different places because no-one could accommodate fifteen people. You would be hard pushed to describe the palm and driftwood shack we stayed in as a hotel. There was no electricity, no running water, beds were wooden pallets with a piece of thick foam covered in a colourful cotton sheet, and a brick would have been more comfortable than the pillows. But we couldn't have cared less. There was a magically replenishing coolbox of beers, sun, sea, sand and— no, sadly none of the other for most of us.

'Lunch?' queried the proprietor, when we asked about food. He thought for a moment. 'Yes, okay. Lunch will come soon.'

We watched as he got into his small wooden boat and headed out to sea with his fishing gear and a young lad to help him.

A couple of days later, on the way back to Stone Town, we stopped at one of the island's famous spice gardens. As we wandered through the aromatic greenery, red colobus monkeys were swinging through the tall trees above us, occasionally stopping to poke their faces through the canopy and look at us with startled curiosity. We lost ourselves in the hot earthy smell of cinnamon and the creamy sweetness of vanilla. We tasted under-ripe green peppercorns, smeared our lips with the red fruit of the achiote plant, and chewed on pungent cloves.

'Do you have any ginger?' I asked.

'Oh yes, all people in Zanzibar love ginger,' said the garden owner.

'Can I buy some, please?'

He went to fetch a piece then offered it to me in his cupped hands.

'It's yours. My gift. You need ginger tea?'

'Thank you,' I said. 'Yes, it's good for seasickness.' I was already fretting about the dreaded return ferry to Dar es Salaam.

'Ah, well, you might not need that,' said Anthony, smiling. He rummaged around in his day pack and came out with a crumpled envelope. 'This is for you from me, John and Mark.'

I think my glass face said it all when I saw a ticket for a twenty-minute light plane flight from Zanzibar to Dar. I could have kissed them. I think I did.

CHAPTER FOURTEEN
In lions I trust

The Ngorongoro Crater is a two-million-year-old geological masterpiece. It's a caldera, the remains of a vast volcano whose last explosion was so intensely powerful that it collapsed in on itself. Today, its sixteen-kilometre-wide arena is ringed by forested slopes which rise about six hundred metres above the mostly flat interior.

We stood at the rim, open-mouthed spectators before this ancient natural amphitheatre. Being the dry season, we watched as dust trails marked the movement of jeeps on the crater floor. We could see a large lake and a few patches of forest punctuating the rolling grasslands. Driving down into the crater in Land Rovers with our driver-guides, it felt like we were leaving time behind and heading into a lost world.

I tried not to care too much whether I saw a lion or not, and was surprised that the first animals we passed were domestic cattle. I hadn't realised that the Maasai could graze their cattle in the park but, of course, this was their land. The warriors guarding the cattle sauntered along, spears in hand and short swords at their side. Clothed in their traditional red shukas and wearing sandals made from old car tyres, they were extensively adorned with belts, necklaces, headdresses and earrings of multi-coloured beads. These tall, lean men with their finely braided long hair were as elegant as any catwalk model and exuded an inner confidence I'd have given my eye teeth for. If they were anxious about predators attacking, they didn't show it. They were at home in this wild place. They knew their land and knew how to look after themselves and their precious cattle.

We, on the other hand, were understandably not allowed out of the vehicles. We drove slowly through the reserve and it was almost shocking to see how much wildlife there was Everywhere we looked, life abounded within the confines of the Crater's green walls. High-pitched barking drew our attention to a herd of zebras having an altercation near a small creek. A huge bull elephant with tusks nearly reaching the ground paraded majestically past some flat-topped acacia trees. A female ostrich startled a family of handsome Thomson's gazelles as she sped by with a male in hot pursuit. In the distance, the shoreline of Lake Magadi was wrapped in a pink feather boa by an aptly named flamboyance of flamingos.

'What's that?'

Someone pointed to a heap of dirty matted fur on the side of the track.

'Is that a dead hyena?' asked Anita.

Our guide, Joyful, stopped by the pitiful mound. It was indeed a bloated hyena with mud- and blood-encrusted fur. It looked like it had been run over.

'Ah,' said Joyful, 'no, this is not a dead hyena.' We looked again. It looked like a hyena to us but then we were novices at this safari lark.

'What is it then?'

'This,' he said, with a serious face, 'is a fat, lazy hyena!' And as he cracked up laughing, the dead thing opened one eye.

'Oh, wait. Listen.' Joyful held up a hand for quiet.

We could hear it. A lion was roaring in the distance. We set off, arriving a few minutes later on a rough track with a wide plain full of wildebeest, zebras and impalas on our right and a low hill of short grasses on our left. We were all scouring the land near the plains game, trying to see whether a lion was hiding, ready to pounce. I don't know who saw him first but, suddenly, there he was. A huge male lion rose up onto the hill on our left, his noble face framed by a magnificent dark mane. Hiding was most certainly not for this impressive specimen. He was in his prime and on a mission and he didn't care who knew it. Completely ignoring us, he looked past our vehicle towards the herds of potential prey, but he wasn't interested in them either. He turned to his right and started walking. Joyful did a quick three-point turn and we shadowed him as he padded through the short grasses. I couldn't help feeling that each time one of his paws touched the earth, a bass drum should have struck a sonorous beat and the ground should have shaken. This king deserved an orchestra. On second thoughts, though, no; he needed nothing. He had everything. His outward beauty was undeniable, his strength and dignity was plain to see, his courage was a given or he wouldn't be where he was today, and his eyes showed an inner power and self-belief — he had no questions, he just was. He knew that this land and his position in it was his birthright.

He was not the only lion we saw that day but he was the one who touched me the most, and he was as close to my wished-for Aslan from Narnia as I could have hoped for. It was quite a while since I'd thought of Rumi, the Sufi poet I learned about back in Turkey, but one of his lines came to me: *Whatever lifts the corners of your mouth, trust that.*

I trusted that lion. I trusted all the wildlife and wilderness around me, and the corners of my mouth were most certainly lifted by them.

We ended the day at Olduvai Gorge, a steep-sided ravine in northern Tanzania's Rift Valley between the Ngorongoro Crater and the Serengeti where we were heading the next day. Olduvai is the place where, in 1960, Mary and Louis Leakey found the fossilized skull of one of our ancient ancestors. It turned out to be key to our understanding of the origins of humankind. Globally important things were found in this vicinity, including many fossilized hominid bones and teeth, stone tools such as hand axes, smaller cutting tools and, not far away, there were even some 3.7-million-year-old footprints. This 'cradle of mankind' was declared a UNESCO World Heritage site in 1979 but despite that, very few people came here. There was a boring excuse of a museum back then. It wasn't really worth the bother unless you were a research scientist. But the location itself most certainly was worth the journey. Apart from the impressive gash in the earth where many of the fossils and ancient artefacts were discovered, there was a huge rock monolith called the Castle which wouldn't have looked out of place in America's Monument Valley. In a few months, I knew this vast area would be a very different and much busier place as the annual wildebeest migration would be returning. Two million animals, mainly wildebeest but also thousands of Thompson's gazelles and many attendant predators, would make their way south from northern Serengeti and the Masai Mara following the rains that brought the lush grasses for them to feed on. A significant number of them would pass this way but they wouldn't reach here until about November.

In mid-September, the distant backdrop of the misty Naibor Soit Hills looked out over a mostly wildlife-free, or at least mammal-free, expanse of rock, grasses, acacia and commiphora (myrrh) trees, and scrubby bushes including the sisal known as *oldupai* in the Maasai language.

But there was a feeling here. An old feeling. A spirit. Perhaps I'm too susceptible to stories and imagination, but out here in the middle of nowhere, I could understand why this was a place of settlement long ago. You could live here . . . if you knew how.

Living here for a night was pretty easy when you had a truck full of equipment, water and food, so that's what we did. We wild camped in this vast expanse of Africa — at Olduvai, one of the world's most ancient camping sites.

Early that evening, everyone seemed to be busy with something — cooking, writing diaries in the truck, chatting with tent-mates or sorting washing — and I found myself sitting alone by the campfire with a bottle of cold beer in hand. I liked quiet moments alone as they were so rare. It was a clear night. The stars were beginning to get their party frocks on and the half moon was low down in the sky. As I spent time reflecting on the past few days and thinking about where I was, what I was doing and how lucky I was, I stared at the impossibly beautiful midnight blue heavens. After about ten minutes, it dawned on me that the moon had moved, not much, but enough to notice if you were looking. And I was. For the first time ever, I was doing nothing but watching the night sky. I sat in silence, transfixed, as the Earth turned and the moon climbed higher. I remained motionless on my camp stool. I hadn't moved but my whole world had shifted. I was flying through the universe on a patch of green canvas, a tiny speck on a fragile planet, no control, no brakes, no power at all.

Time stopped. I was inconsequential. The experience was both liberating and magical. I was in the wilderness of the dark continent, at the 'cradle of mankind', and I saw the moon rise for the first time in my life. It was like being given a gift. For the second time that day, Africa grabbed hold of my heart and gave it a good shake.

The Serengeti is about the size of Belgium and its name comes from a Maasai word meaning 'endless plains'. The Maasai chose the name perfectly as, unlike the Ngorongoro Crater where the boundaries are obvious, once you are in the middle of the Serengeti you see no end to it. It feels as if there is no other Africa than this eternal sea of grass interrupted by outcrops of huge granite boulders, a few life-bringing rivers, acacia woodlands and the occasional ancient baobab tree, where a cornucopia of wondrous wild things live their lives undisturbed by mankind.

If only. The reality is that, along with most of Earth's natural ecosystems, the Serengeti and its inhabitants are under intense pressure from human activity. At the time, though, I didn't recognise the extent of the danger and I felt no concern for the animals we encountered. I saw only the beauty we were surrounded by. Twelve elegant giraffes sauntered along in slow-motion, while, rounding a clump of bushes, we surprised a family of warthogs who barrelled off across the savannah with their upright tails flagging their progress through the long grasses. Closer to the track, a crotchety-looking male buffalo shook his head to dislodge a naughty oxpecker who was attacking an open wound on his neck. Something that looked like a small rock kopje set in the arid golden plains transformed into a rhino when he put his head up from grazing. Five hippos wallowed and yawned in a disgustingly rank pool. A leopard was perched in a spindly acacia tree having invited an impala for lunch. And just ahead of us, a lioness led two small cubs across the dirt track. We watched them with awe and melting hearts.

We spent that night at a campsite in the middle of the Serengeti. It had been a dawn start to the day, so after dinner we all soon headed to our tents for an early night. At some point in the night, I was awoken. It was still pitch black and I was unsure what had stirred me from my sleep. I listened in case someone in the camp had called for help. All was quiet. As I was drifting back into slumber, a lion called from far away.

'Mraaa. Mraaa, mraa, aa, aa.'

This deep, ancient voice rolled like a golden wave across the sea of grass and crashed into my chest. I had no hope of survival — I was lost to the spell of the wilderness. Oh-oh, the corners of my mouth were lifting again.

CHAPTER FIFTEEN
Friends and family

Three days later we were in Nairobi and it was the end of this first leg of the trip. We said sad goodbyes to most of the group but some were still around for a few days. John, Anita, Evelyn and Nicky were waiting for the second section to begin. Freddie and I now had our work cut out getting prepared for the next trip starting in a week's time.

First things first, though, I had to get to the *poste restante*. Would there be a letter from Guy? He might have got my letter from Victoria Falls, but then, he might not. Trying to communicate from different continents whilst we were both constantly on the move . . . well, it added a whole new layer to the difficulty generally associated with long-distance relationships. But then, did we actually have a relationship?

My heart was in my mouth as I waited for the lady at the post office to return to the desk. Yes! Yes, yes, yes. She passed me a small airmail envelope. And yes! It was from Guy. I dashed outside into the warm sun, found a spot under a jacaranda tree, and opened his letter.

Turkey, 3rd September 1990
Dear Amanda
So you got this letter!

Isn't Kenya great? But the real fun is yet to come for you. You'll love it.

My trip is very different. Only eight passengers, and the Gulf War is causing us a lot of headaches. We can't go to Jordan or Syria and the Brits can't get visas for Iran which is a bit of a spoiler.

Yve is a nice girl, but she's not you. I'm missing you a lot. I hated the way we left each other at Heathrow but I didn't know what to say and I don't think you did either. It was certainly easier than a big scene but still bloody difficult. We've picked a strange way of life where we have to put ourselves through these sorts of emotional pressures. I hope we can see each other soon, even though I know it's not possible with our planned itineraries. I don't even know if you want to see me again, or more to the point will want to when the time comes in God knows how many months or years.

Anyway, I hope you're having a good time on your trip and maybe even find someone to give you companionship. I'm seeing things I've never seen before, really looking forward to Pakistan, India and Nepal, and still enjoying the way of life and managing to have a beer or six.
I'll write to you at your next post stop. Maybe I'll even get a letter from you?
All I really want to say is I hope you're having a fantastic time, and to let you know I'm missing you masses.
With love, Guy xxx

He was missing me! Masses! And he wanted to see me again. I was sitting under the tree grinning like one of the hyenas we'd seen last week. I'd spent the last two months trying to convince myself that I should expect nothing from Guy, but here it was, in writing, that I *could* keep him close to my heart. If nothing else, it looked like I'd be writing more letters to him. Since I couldn't share my adventure with him in person, I would share it on paper.

A little later that morning, I checked in at the place where we picked up faxes from the Drago-office and there was yet more communication from Guy. He'd sent a note to the UK office to be forwarded to me here. The message was brief, quite impersonal, and hugely unexpected.

> *Hi Amanda, I hope you're OK and got my letter· Can I ask you to do me a big favour? I've just found out that my folks are in Nairobi for the next two days at The Norfolk Hotel· Could you buy them a bottle of bubbly from me and take it round to their hotel as a surprise from me? I'll sort the money with Drago· If you manage to meet them, please tell them I'm fine and send my love· Thanks, I'd appreciate it· Guy·*

Meeting the parents of someone you like is usually a bit of a milestone in a relationship, isn't it? But normally, you'd expect your partner to be there and you'd generally assume the meeting would take place in the country where you lived. Still, this wasn't really about 'meeting the parents' and Guy wasn't my partner, it was just about doing a favour for a friend. Truth be told, though, I was fascinated to have a chance to meet them. I decided to head off straight away, knowing that I would be busy the next day.

I sat down and waited as the receptionist rang up to their room.

'Good morning, Mr Marks. You have a visitor here. She says to say that Guy sent her.'

The immediately noticeable thing about Donald was that the right side of his face drooped. A stroke? Bell's palsy? Whatever it was, over lunch I discovered that it didn't stop him from being a real joker. I could see where Guy got his easy and often cheeky banter from. Daphne, a recently retired consultant anaesthetist, was utterly charming and very curious about this young woman who had been sent by her son. She was obviously missing Guy and was already looking forward to flying to Kathmandu to see him in a few months. A posh lunch in an upmarket hotel, a lovely conversation about travel and Guy . . . for a couple of hours, it felt like 'normal' life. I even got a hug from Daphne. The visit made me feel closer to Guy but I also felt further away from my own family. By coincidence, my mum would be in Nairobi in just over a week, but we'd have left by then. Close, but just not close enough.

Nairobi, 17th September 1990
Dear Guy
Yes, I got your letter. Is it bad of me to say that I'm very pleased you're missing me? I'm also glad you mentioned about us leaving at Heathrow. You're right, I didn't know what to say at the airport. I was miserable and in my miserableness I decided that you were indifferent. If you hadn't written this letter I'm sure I wouldn't have written much more than my last (first) tentative letter. I'm a coward and don't let feelings out lightly. In fact, I cried nearly the whole flight to Harare. Silly, I know. Anyway, you might gather from this that

I'm missing you a touch. And as for companionship, well, there are plenty of the group who are great to be with, and Freddie too of course, but no, no-one special. Who knows when we'll see each other again. Anything's possible, but we both know how things are — difficult. Your folks are lovely people. Your dad's a bit of a character, isn't he? They took me for lunch, which was very sweet of them. It was so strange spending time with people I've never met before and yet we both have you in common. Were your ears burning? They should have been!

Thursday 20th September
Well, things have changed over the last few days. It's turned out that I have a week in Nairobi by myself. Freddie and the truck have left for an impromptu trip around Kenyan game parks with a mix of passengers on layover here including some of our next group. I've been left here for a week to wait for Central African Republic visas. The embassy is just not playing ball and I'm having to go along with their games and wait in queues each day to find that, yet again, no visas have been issued. It's infuriating, especially as my giardia has returned and I'm feeling pretty average and need to be in reasonable proximity of a loo at all times. Still more annoying, Freddie forgot to leave me money, so I'm hungry and I can't go to the doctor's to get antibiotics as I can't pay for them. Luckily, Sykes is coming here tomorrow, though, so I'm going to hit him for dinner and money. It'll be good to hear the gossip from the workshop. Plus,

Hoggy and Jimbo arrive here on Sunday with their group (they're leading the southbound Cairo to Harare trip), so I've booked both of our groups into Carnivore's that night. Line up the dawas!

Anyway we'll be leaving here about eight days late now because of the CAR visas, and one really brilliant thing about that is that I get to see my Mum as she arrives here with her friend on a trip on 28th for two days. Seems it's the done thing to come to Nairobi at the moment. I can't wait to see her.

Lastly, we've heard some worrying news about Zaire. Apparently the road department which does the grading and pothole filling has been disbanded. We were told that the roads are in an atrocious state, and of course, we'll hit Zaire in the rain. Looks like fun times ahead.

I don't suppose you'd like to fly out to Zaire in your two weeks off in Kathmandu would you?

I miss you.

Much love, Amanda xx

'Sykes' was Mike Sykes, the third owner of Dragoman alongside G and Charlie. He was in Kenya on a bit of a holiday but taking the opportunity to say hi to some of the crew in Nairobi. Sykes did indeed buy me dinner and give me enough money to tide me over and buy my much-needed antibiotics. He was also delighted to be joining the party at Carnivores on Sunday. No traveller could miss the institution that was Carnivores — unless you were a vegetarian. The restaurant was famous for its huge open barbecue pits where haunches of giraffe, zebra, crocodile and countless other game meats were roasted to perfection before being offered to diners from long Maasai spears that were taken around the tables by the chefs. I wasn't sure what I felt about eating some of the animals we'd only recently watched roaming freely but I was willing to accept the promises that the meat came from ethical sources. It was a fun night of laughs, stories and reminiscing thanks to the great company, delicious food and the unmissable *dawas*. *Dawa* is the Swahili word for medicine and this drink was a very quaffable but lethal concoction of cane spirit, honey and lime juice.

'So, I gather Guy is missing you,' said Sykes at some point that evening. He must have been dying to ask me this since we met earlier in the week but it took the *dawas* to encourage him to ask. Sykes liked a good gossip as much as the rest of us, even if he was the boss.

'Really?' I said, blushing like an idiot. 'Well, I'm pleased to hear it. So he should be!'

Now who told him that, I wondered?

It was such a busy and unexpectedly sociable couple of weeks that it seemed to go by very fast. I managed to get some rest in a decent bed, so with that and the medication, by the end of our stay I was feeling pretty good. What made Nairobi particularly memorable for me, though, was meeting up with my mum the day before we left. She and her friend, Dorothy, had come for a long-wished-for safari and she had no idea that I would still be in the city when she came back from Tsavo. Having rung Dad earlier in the week, I realised I could spring a surprise on her in Nairobi, so, late on our last afternoon, I headed over to her hotel. Discovering that their coach was yet to arrive, I waited in reception. How odd to be doing this yet again, I thought. First with Guy's parents and now with Mum.

I saw her before she saw me. She was chatting away to Dorothy, her bright, beautiful, sun-tanned face beaming as they came into the hotel with their small group.

'So, did you have a good time on safari, Mrs Hewitt?' I said, coming up behind her.

She turned. 'Oh yes, we— Oh! Oh!' Tears sprang to her eyes, her hand flew to her mouth and she dropped her bag at her feet. 'Oh, Mand.' She grabbed me and hugged me so tightly I thought I'd burst. 'My little girl. You're here. How? Oh, I'm so happy. Dorothy, did you know? Does your dad know? But you shouldn't be here. Is anything wrong? Are you ill?'

We cried, we laughed, we hugged. I answered all her questions and we chatted non-stop throughout the evening over a dinner of 'Chicken in a basket without the basket' (it honestly said that on the menu). I told her about my trip so far, they told me about their safari, and I heard all the news from home. You know the kind of thing, normal family stuff: Nana and Grandma were well, my sister Sam wasn't enjoying her job, Dad's knee was playing up, Jester our English setter was as bonkers as ever. I was such a long way from home but for that evening I was right back there and it felt warm and cosy and wonderfully familiar.

Very little in my life was familiar these days which was both one of the joys and one of the challenges of travel for me. Stepping out of my comfort zone opened my eyes to the unknown and the unexpected, the beautiful and the ugly both in the world around me and in myself. This precious evening with Mum gave me a night off my long journey, but it also made me realise how many unforgettable experiences I'd already had and just how much I'd changed. As well as finding the wild lions I'd longed to see, I'd rafted the Zambezi from the foot of Victoria Falls, explored ancient tombs and underground cities, danced with Maasai, taken tea with Bedouins, swum in the Indian Ocean, trekked in the foothills of Mount Kilimanjaro . . . The timid, self-conscious young woman who worked in an advertising agency two years earlier was gone. After six months in Egypt and the Middle East and two months in East and Southern Africa, I was feeling more at home in this complicated world of diverse cultures, beliefs, values and behaviours. I was still a work in progress but I was proud of myself for coming this far. I'd gone from shiny bum to grease monkey, from trainee co-driver to tour leader, and maybe one day I'd be the confident overland expedition leader I now half-believed I could be. I was reasonably proficient at most aspects of truck maintenance, and driving on the mostly untarred roads of East Africa hadn't fazed me. I was aware, though, that Zaire was looming. I was half-terrified and half-excited at the prospect but there was no backing out now. We were off tomorrow.

As I said goodbye to Mum that night, I was leaving home again. But I had two treasured things to carry with me through the next four and a half months of adventure: a big hug from Mum and the knowledge that Guy was missing me.

CHAPTER SIXTEEN
Drummers, muggers and pearl fishers

'Bloody hell, we must be expecting visitors — Jeremy Joe's put clean clothes on!'

Nicky stood at the cook table, kettle in hand. 'We're honoured, Joe. Morning coffee, sir? Don't spill it!'

This British solicitor turned African adventurer had quickly embraced overlanding's required *laissez-faire* attitude to cleanliness. Meticulous hand washing and food hygiene was something all leaders beat into any new group, but other than that, well, what's a bit of mud and muck between friends? In fact, all my trips so far had mostly allowed for keeping pretty clean and tidy if you wanted to but, travelling further west and north into central Africa, things were about to change as we left behind so-called civilisation and facilities on tap.

I liked Jeremy from the off. He was lovable, very funny, a bit naughty, really good company and he liked a chat. He had one of those faces which made you trust everything he said — probably quite a good trait for a solicitor. I haven't the foggiest idea how we came to call him Jeremy Joe but it suited him.

Jeremy grinned at the people already sitting around on stools enjoying a good breakfast of porridge and fresh fruit. He added his luggage to the growing pile of bags on the tarpaulin by the back locker and accepted the proffered red melamine cup. Jeremy was our fire-wallah — crucial on this journey if we were to eat well —but he hadn't been needed that morning. He'd chosen one of the more demanding wallahships because he was determined to get stuck in and get fit. Ali, Freddie's girlfriend who also joined us in Nairobi, was a fabulous cook and she'd already warned Jeremy that she'd be needing some good, long-lasting fires so she could bake bread and cakes for us all.

'You're right about the clothes,' said Jeremy. 'I probably shouldn't have bothered yet, but you know, can't let standards drop just because we're in the wild. You're welcome to take a leaf out of my book any time, Nicky.'

It was early morning at Seronera in the middle of the Serengeti and we were about five days into the trip. For those of us who'd come from Harare, it felt like this was the true start of our new adventure as, since leaving Nairobi, we'd been retracing our steps. Today was our last chance to enjoy the huge expanses of East Africa's savannah lands and the animals which called them home, as we would be driving straight through the middle of the park and exiting by the western gate for a night at Fort Ikoma. We were on our way to Burundi via Lake Victoria before entering Zaire. We were on a roll, or at least we were until we hit the black cotton soil. In the dry season, this type of soil bakes rock hard and cracks into everyone's stereotypical idea of a parched African landscape, a perfect theme for a sadistic jigsaw puzzle maker. However, black cotton is a rather Jekyll and Hyde substance, and as far as drivers are concerned, Mr Hyde shows his face in the rainy season. Imagine trying to drive through thick wet clay mixed with black treacle and you'll have some idea of why truck drivers aren't too keen on this type of soil when it's sodden. So far in my overlanding career I'd only ever got stuck in the sands of Wadi

Rum in Jordan where sand-matting had been quite good fun. Here, our steel mats were rechristened 'mud mats' and getting bogged was a whole different kettle of fish.

We were only about a mile from Serengeti's western exit gate when Freddie tried to drive around a broken-down vehicle. Within a few feet of leaving the road, we were up to our axles in black cotton. There was nothing for it, we had to dig. Along with Ali, I ended up under the back of the truck for at least an hour trying to dig out the buried differential, part of the back axle, while others tried to release the front wheels from the grip of the black stuff. A few of the group stood around looking on, either not willing to get mucky or perhaps not yet realising that this journey was all about teamwork and self-reliance. No-one was going to be coming to get us out of whatever sticky situations we got ourselves into. For weeks on end, not a soul would know exactly where we were, and Freddie and I couldn't do all the work alone. An African overland expedition was an all-hands-on-deck effort, never more so than on this upcoming long journey from western Tanzania through to Morocco.

'You did this on purpose, Freddie, didn't you?' said Jeremy Joe, now plastered in black mud. 'You know, if my clean clothes bothered you that much, you only had to say so.'

Freddie laughed. 'Sorry, mate. This is good training, though. It's nothing compared to what we're going to be going through in Zaire. Then, we'll get bloody brilliant at digging!'

Freddie seemed to be relishing the prospect of Zaire but I had mixed feelings about it having heard all the stories of dreadful roads with huge mud holes. How was I going to cope with driving through things like that? It was a daunting thought. But it was the kind of adventure I'd come for and Freddie would be there to advise me. All overland leaders learned from the previous leader, ensuring that skills and knowledge were passed on. It would be fine. Surely?

Eventually escaping the gloopy grasp of Serengeti's mud, that evening we were lucky to have a half-decent campsite where we could get ourselves clean. The next day we continued west through Tanzania, taking a roll-on-roll-off ferry across a short stretch of Lake Victoria from Mwanza to Busisi, and soon entered the tiny country of Burundi.

Burundi was one of the most beautiful countries I'd travelled through. It was a magical landscape of closely packed, intensely cultivated green hills. The scent of pine permeated the countryside air. Alongside the many pines were eucalyptus and jacaranda trees interspersed with bananas, coffee plants and flame trees. Nothing was monotone. There were no huge fields. All was higgledy-piggledy and Jackson Pollocky.

From my outsider's point of view, I loved the fact that nature still seemed to have enough of a say here to keep things diverse and quirky, but of course the beauty I saw hid a multitude of problems which, as someone simply passing through, I didn't have the time to come to know or understand. I didn't see Hutus and Tutsis walking down the earth roads carrying piles of logs or a stalk of green bananas on their head, I saw Burundians. I didn't recognise the mass deforestation because I was distracted by the diverse small-scale agriculture. I didn't see people on the edge of hunger trying to subsist from what they could grow on their tiny patchwork scraps of land, I saw happy smiling faces and laughing children running alongside our truck. Perhaps that sounds like blind ignorance but we had a matter of days here and no chance to stop and truly learn. One of the downsides of a long overland journey like this was that you never had long enough to get properly under the skin of any place. On the positive side, though, if you were curious enough, you ended up having a decent general knowledge about a lot of countries. For some travellers, that was enough, for others, it was a useful starting point.

We made a short unplanned visit to Karera Falls on our way to Bujumbura, the capital of Burundi. Freddie was always keen to fit in as much as possible. We wished we hadn't bothered, though, as we came across some unfortunately aggressive officials who objected to us bringing Huwey into their car park. An argument ensued.

'Excuse me, sir.' A man in a suit came over to Freddie after seeing our altercation. 'I am very sorry for the welcome you have had here. I give you my apology. Travellers are always welcome in Burundi. May I make amends to you and your friends?'

'Thanks,' said Freddie, 'but there's no need. We'll just take a quick look at the falls and go.'

'I would hate you to leave Burundi with bad memories. Please, I would like to invite you all to a special performance. I am the minister for tourism.'

Well, we weren't expecting that!

'Oh, right,' said Freddie, shaking the man's hand. 'A performance, you say?'

'Yes, of the Royal Drummers of Burundi.'

'No! Really? They have a performance nearby?'

'I am inviting you to a private performance at Gishora Hill in Gitega. Just for you and your friends. Will you come? This afternoon? I will meet you there.'

We couldn't believe our luck. The actual Royal Drummers of

Burundi. Sometimes you just have to be in the right place at the right time. It seems that an abortive visit to Karera Falls was our unexpected ticket to a gig by these world-famous musicians.

On the top of a hill in the middle of Africa, in front of a stage of dusty red earth and grass, we heard the drummers before we saw them. Twenty drummers entered their home-turf arena dressed in robes of red, white and green, the colours of the country's flag, each with a huge and very heavy-looking drum on their head. They were beating the wooden belly and the animal hide top of their drums with two wooden sticks as they jumped, kicked and sang their way in front of us.

Ba da dum da da dum da da dum da. Ba da dum da da dum da da dum da.

Sitting between Freddie and myself, our host explained that the drums were made of the hollowed-out tree trunks of the *umuvugangoma* tree.

'The word means *the tree that makes the drums speak*. This tree is only in Burundi. These drums are sacred and they are handed down through the generations from father to son. That drum in the middle,' he said, pointing to a very large painted drum which had been placed in the middle of the semi-circle, 'that is the lead drum, the *inkiryana*. You know, it is a huge privilege to be a Royal Drummer even now that the performances are no longer for our royal family. Both Hutus and Tutsis come together here.'

The minister seemed proud to say this, and well he might as, since independence in 1962, Burundi had been plagued by ethnic conflict between the minority yet more dominant Tutsis and the more populous but generally less wealthy Hutus. A Hutu uprising in 1972 saw around 200,000 Hutus massacred by government forces, and again in 1988 Tutsis slaughtered

132

thousands of Hutus and caused many more thousands to flee to Rwanda. Sadly, yet to come, 1993 would bring the country yet more horrors, as Hutus slaughtered thousands of Tutsis, and in neighbouring Rwanda, 1994 would see an even more widespread genocide which would appal the world. Genocide is not a pretty word and peace was fragile in Burundi. If this drumming was beating a rhythm of reconciliation as well as joy then it was significant indeed.

Some of the drummers kept a constant beat, others took on the main pattern of the song, and then all the group took a solo turn on the *inkiryana*. But this was not just skilful drumming. This was an energetic feast of rhythm and song and dance, a celebration of chanting, shouting, spinning and leaping. And you could tell they weren't just doing this because their government minister had asked them to, they were obviously loving it every bit as much as we were. Their smiles were for each other as much as us. They were connected, sharing and savouring the music and the moment. Their exuberance and happiness were infectious. The thunderous sounds vibrated my whole body, and yet there was also something hypnotic and almost meditative about the performance. Who knew that drumming could be so complex?

We left our perch on the top of Burundi feeling on top of the world.

Two days later, walking back from Bujumbura town, Anita and I could see the gates of the yacht club at the end of the long tree-lined road. We were nearly back at camp. Four young men sauntered out from a field at the side of the road and headed in our direction. We thought nothing of them and carried on chatting as we walked. We smiled as we were about to pass them.

133

They stopped.

'Jambo,' said a tall, skinny one with legs up to his armpits. He had a wide smile and friendly eyes but his companions seemed distinctly less agreeable.

'Hi,' we replied, as we went to sidestep them and continue down the road. But the tall man put his hand on my arm and stopped me. Immediately, Anita screamed and ran off down the road towards the camp. Quick thinking. I should have done that. In seconds, the hand had tightened its grip on my arm and I was going nowhere.

'Give me the bag,' said the man, still smiling.

I had a small black bum bag slung over my shoulder instead of discreetly tied around my waist as it should have been. What a fool I was. I should have known better. I always warned groups to be ultra-careful about carrying things safely when they were out and about, and yet here I was taking precisely none of my own advice. Careless. In the midst of this hot African city on the shore of Lake Tanganyika, I was immediately transported back to that snowy day in Leeds four-and-a-half years ago. This was not going to happen again.

'No, absolutely not,' I said, looking him in the face while struggling to free my arm. The other men just stood there watching.

Tall-man wasn't taking 'no' for an answer, though. He made a grab for my bag. Perhaps I should have been frightened, but actually I was just angry. I'd become quite strong for my size over the last couple of years, and he probably wasn't expecting a fight. I yanked it away from him. He pulled it back. I held on. It must have looked quite comical from a distance. A six-and-a half-foot man playing close-quarters tug-of-war with a five-foot-two woman. We did a few rounds of to-ing and fro-ing until the man had obviously had enough of this annoying little woman who wouldn't give in, so he brought up one of his stupidly long legs to my stomach and pushed. I fell over, still hanging on to my bag, and was dragged a short way before the bag was inevitably snatched from my grip.

'Aaagh!' I yelled, as the men fled leaving me at the side of the road shouting obscenities at them. 'Give it back. You bastaaards!'

So that was my second mugging. Not so silent this time and, oddly enough, not so frightening, though it probably should have been. They got away with ten dollars, a cheap watch I rarely wore, and my prescription sunglasses. I thought I would be most upset about my sunnies but actually I was far more outraged by my obvious helplessness in the face of their assault. I was spitting chips and shaking — cross with myself and mad as hell at them. How dare they. How bloody dare they! Aaagh!

I wanted to keep screaming at them but it was pointless. I had no choice but to give up. They'd gone. I walked down the road towards the yacht club, meeting Anita's rescue party running up the road towards me.

I knew I had to let it go, but thoughts kept going round and round my head all afternoon and into the evening.

'I should have kept my bag hidden.'

Yes, that was stupid. Too late. Get over it, don't do it again.

'What if they'd had a knife or a gun?'

But they didn't. They were just chancers. You're okay.

'I should have run immediately.'

You couldn't. He was holding onto to you, remember?

'They could have hurt me if they'd decided to.'

Yes, they could have but they didn't. You're safe.

'What if I'd had the truck keys in my bag?'

You didn't. They were round your neck, as always.

'I should have fought harder.'

Now you're being silly. You did fight. You did what you could. Enough.

'Why me? Again.'

Hmm. I don't know. But never again. No-one is ever going to do that to you again.

I sat alone in the cab until quite late that night, my frustrations flowing from my pen nib until they calmed and dried along with the ink. Poor Guy, he probably didn't deserve that outpouring so I probably wouldn't send the letter. I put a tape in the cab stereo. Very quietly, my mum wrapped her arms around me in the form of one of her favourite songs, 'Au fond du temple saint', a duet from Bizet's *The Pearl Fishers* opera by Jussi Bjoerling and Robert Merrill. The moon glittered on the gentle waves of Lake Tanganyika, a hippo wandered past the truck, and I went to bed, happy again. Tomorrow we would hit Zaire. Bring it on!

CHAPTER SEVENTEEN
Zaire

'Hey guys,' began Freddie as always, 'If you can listen up, I just want to tell you a bit more about the next few weeks.'

It was our first night in Goma, Zaire, or rather in a turkey farm by the lake just outside of town. The ex-pat farm owners kindly offered overlanders a safe place to stop and relax for a night or two. The rain had stopped, we'd all managed to get a lukewarm shower, and Jeremy had a good campfire going.

'So, it's about fifteen hundred miles from here to where we leave Zaire. We're already running a week late thanks to the Central African Republic giving us the runaround on visas, but I was still hoping to get through before the rains hit us. The trans-African highway is . . . well, highway is a bit of a grand word for this crater-ridden obstacle course. The roads you've seen so far are nothing to what we'll get further on. On a good run in the dry season, our trucks can get through Zaire in maybe three weeks. But . . . Amanda and I have heard that the roads department isn't working because they've not been paid for months and there are already reports of extremely churned up roads and long truck blockages at the really bad bogholes. I think it could take us at least four weeks. This isn't going to be easy. But then, you didn't come for easy, did you?'

A cheer of agreement went up. Everyone was well and truly

up for the adventure. No backup, no communication. We were on our own. We had a truck, a map, some route notes and a Freddie. What more could we need?

'Honestly,' he continued, 'it'll be great fun. I just want to flag up a couple of important things. As of tomorrow, washing water is rationed. You can only have one washing-up bowl of water a night unless there's a very good reason for needing more. Also, I need you to look out for each other more than normal. If anyone is feeling ill, you tell Anita and Evelyn or me and Amanda. That can be if you're feeling mentally unwell or anxious too. There was one passenger I heard about who decided that they'd had enough of Zaire and set off for home on foot. The group had to tie them up for a while to stop them fighting to escape. They were on Larium pills for malaria and some people say they can make you paranoid. So please, if anything's not right, talk. Keep wounds as clean as possible or they might turn into tropical ulcers. Believe me, that's a very bad thing. Oh, and talking about wounds, you need to know about jiggers.'

Oh hell. I'd heard graphic horror stories about these critters back in the workshop but I'd forgotten all about them until Freddie mentioned them. A jigger is a type of tropical sand-flea that burrows into your skin and lays its eggs in you. You tend not to notice until the area begins to itch or becomes sore as the eggs develop and grow.

'It's most common to find them in your feet,' he said, 'even under your toenails, but they can lay anywhere, so be aware. Seriously, check yourselves out.'

'We have scalpels at the ready,' said Evelyn, one of the nurses in the group, with a grin.

The group suddenly realised this wasn't a joke.

'Well, if you've got them, wherever they are, they need to come out,' said Evelyn, 'otherwise infections can set in and we really don't want that. And don't worry if they're in an awkward place, boys, Anita and I have seen it all before and we won't laugh . . . much.'

Goma felt like a town on the edge of existence. Life is bound to be rather precarious when you're only ten miles from Mount Nyiragongo, one of the world's most active volcanoes — a volcano that has a huge lava lake whose contents have been known to race down its steep sides like water, at speeds of up to forty miles an hour. Nyirangongo's lava flow destroyed the lives of hundreds of people in 1977 and would again in 2002. When you add Lake Kivu into the mix, it's quite surprising that anyone lives here at all. Kivu is a deep lake with a deadly secret: poisonous volcanic gases are dissolved in the lower strata of its clear waters. One day, the lake itself could explode.

Even though Goma has an almost post-apocalyptic feel to it, in between eruptions, the slopes of the volcano are covered with lush foliage and you find lilies and hibiscus thriving amongst the black rocks. The area is actually very beautiful.

The town's main street was somewhat reminiscent of a set from an old cowboy film: a wide road flanked by colonnaded yet very run-down shops slightly raised on either side and relatively few vehicles. They didn't have much but they had fabric shops. Ali and I revelled in them and bought many lengths of gaudy-coloured cotton to have made into dresses and baggy pants when we next came across a tailor. I mean, every girl needs a dress with a print of the Zairean president's head on, don't they?

Freddie had arranged to change some black-market money

with a man in town — enough to get us through to Kisangani on the Congo River, our roughly halfway point. There was no point changing too many dollars as the inflation rate was spiralling. Our clandestine meeting was on a not-very-secret corner of the main street and our man was counting out our zaires, the name of the currency as well as the country, when we heard shouting coming our way. It didn't feel good.

'Freddie, look.' I nodded towards the ragged rows of khaki-clad soldiers filing into the main street singing and dancing, shouting and swinging their guns around.

'Time to get out of Dodge?' he said, grinning, but with a wary look in his eye.

'I think so.'

'Come on, let's round up our troops, buy that diesel and go and see some gorillas.'

22nd October 1990
Goma, Zaire

Dear Mum and Dad
I know my last letter from Burundi said no more letters until we got to Central African Republic but a passenger is leaving us early to go home to the UK shortly so you've got a surprise extra one!

Well, Zaire has been an eye-opener already. The roads are atrocious and it's raining hard most afternoons so the ground is super soggy. We nearly slipped off the road once already but we're getting very good at fitting the tyre chains on the front and back wheels now, and dab hands at the mud mats too. We're all now constantly covered in red mud, and water is rationed so it looks like we'll be pretty filthy until we get out of Zaire.

Still, at the moment we're all in good spirits because we can still get good food including meat and vegetables, strawberries, wine and even chocolate. I don't think it's going to last long though as in about a week we hit the really bad roads which we're all dreading. I'm already driving with my heart in my mouth each day even though we're often only doing about twenty miles per hour on average. The adrenalin speeds round your body when you see these huge gashes in the road and inclines and mud holes coming up. I'm terrified I'm going to get the truck properly stuck. It feels so good when you've got through it, though. Zaire is definitely a challenge.

Everybody is still very healthy, including me. I'm even putting on weight at last, so don't worry about me. Life has slowed right down now and there's no longer much to see or visit. Instead, we just live in the moment each day and move on each morning. However, yesterday was different. I actually saw mountain gorillas.

We set off at 6 a.m and trekked through the dense jungle of Virunga National Park with a guide at the front with a huge machete clearing a way for us. A lot of the hike was through thick stretches of bamboo forest. It took us until 11.30 to find the gorillas by which time we were all completely knackered. But when you see them · · · oh, it's just so worth the effort. They were just sitting there

141

in a small clearing in the undergrowth — a huge silverback, two females, a young male and a tiny baby· We went far closer than I imagined we would and just sat with them· The baby was prancing about and showing off, and at one point came right up to Evelyn and sniffed her knee· One of the young males put his hand on Greg's knee for a while and another pushed me into a thicket of nettles (gently, but still) to reach some bamboo· You're not supposed to get close, of course, because they are susceptible to our diseases, and we tried not to under the guidance of the rangers, but when you're backed into a bush, there's not much you can do, so the rangers just tell you to sit still and don't look them in the eye· Heart-pounding moments! The silverback didn't seem to mind any of this and just lay down watching us with his head in his hands· We stayed nearly an hour with them but it seemed like ten minutes·

Then we had a five-hour walk back in the torrential rain· I could have sung all the way! I'd do it again tomorrow if I could· I think that's one of the most magical hours I'll ever have in my life· You look at their hands and they're so like ours· And their eyes · · · well, you just know that you're looking at one of our ancestors· You can see the intelligence and the emotion· How anyone can kill such a creature to make ashtrays out of their hands, or eat them · · · I just can't get my head around it· It's like cannibalism· Our guide told us there are only about three hundred mountain gorillas left now· I'm so lucky to have seen them but I'm devastated to think we might lose them·

Today we've had a pretty easy, no-driving day. We camped near some waterfalls and had a major truck clean. It was bliss when, at 5 p.m all the girls trooped off to a secluded spot on the river and all stripped off for a delicious wash. Clean at last, what a wonderful feeling! We'd been about five days without a proper wash. I hate the thought of getting into my dirty sleeping bag now but I don't have much choice. Never mind, I can wash clothes tomorrow after we've done the oil change and other jobs on the truck. Freddie and I have a day just waiting for the group as they're going to see chimpanzees. Sadly, there aren't enough spaces for us. Maybe next trip.

Yesterday we had to mend a short bridge over a river before we could cross it. Actually, I'm not sure you can call what we were faced with a bridge. Two thick tree trunks straddled the river but there was a huge gap between them. There were a couple of planks across the gaping hole but these hadn't made the bridge look any more inviting. I got the feeling that the drivers of big trucks had become so used to seeing bridges like these that they just trusted to God and the fact that the riverbed wasn't strewn with the vehicle carcasses, lined up their wheels and shut their eyes. That wasn't really a tactic we felt comfortable with, so we got out the saws and axes and chopped and scavenged for enough smallish trees to lay across the big trunks. We all stayed out of the truck when Freddie drove across, and there was a big cheer when he reached the other side. Freddie says we'll get good at that by the time we leave

143

Zaire - and apparently, it's my turn to drive over the next one!

I'm learning so much and enjoying myself most of the time. Can't be bad! Miss you all heaps.
Lots of squeaky clean love
Amanda xx

I fell head over heels with the lush, messy beauty of eastern Zaire's forested hills and valleys criss-crossed by boisterous streams and wild rivers. Beneath the tall trees, riotous undergrowth tumbled onto the road and spilled out onto the riverbanks. Nothing was organised or tidy and there was no concrete and tarmac to be seen. We were driving on red earth roads through a tapestry of emerald to olive greenery. At regular intervals, the land had been cleared to make room for round wood and thatch huts surrounded by small gardens. There was always something for sale by the roadside, from avocados to pineapples and charcoal to peanuts, usually at a tiny makeshift wooden stall with a grass roof to keep the sun off the produce. Children waved at us from morning until night — excited faces, bare feet, ragged clothes — some shouting 'Bic' in the hope of being given a pen, others just screaming with delight when we waved back at them.

We'd seen very little that was even close to modern infrastructure outside of Goma and Rutshuru and, being a card-carrying nature lover, I thought this was utterly wonderful. Of course, mine was a privileged point of view. Your average Zairean might have given their right arm for a comfortable life in a small semi in Sunderland. Or maybe not, as Zaireans are proud people, a lesson Jeremy Joe was taught very eloquently by a young man whose fruit and vegetable stall we stopped at one day.

'Hello,' said Jeremy to the very serious-looking man. 'Do you speak any English?'

'I am a man,' said the man, looking almost haughtily at Jeremy.

Jeremy smiled. 'What a coincidence. So am I!'

The man wasn't impressed. 'Yes, but I am a black man.'

That was Jeremy Joe put in his place.

Zaire was a francophone country and one of the largest and most populous countries in Africa. It was also a country whose people were being driven into desperate poverty by their self-styled 'Father of the Nation', and whose buildings, systems and facilities were crumbling by the day. Mobutu Sese Seko Kuku Ngbendu Wa Za Banga means something like "the all-conquering warrior who goes from conquest to conquest". I guess modesty isn't a common trait for any dictator. Mobutu had seized power in a military coup in 1965. Forcing through a campaign of what he called pro-African 'authenticity' in 1971, he renamed Congo as Zaire and forbade any citizen from taking a European name or wearing European-style suits. Mobutu Sese Seko was all about force; that plus violence, corruption, exploitation, greed, excess, nepotism . . . And while his people were abandoned and abused, he pocketed billions of dollars of international aid. Strutting his stuff in his trademark leopard-skin, brimless hat and Mao-style abacost suit, he chartered Concorde to take him shopping in Paris, and he built a palace, his very own 'Versailles in the jungle' at Gbadolite, complete with his own airport. He also organised for an international boxing match to take place in Kinshasa in 1974, the world heavyweight championship between George Foreman and Muhammed Ali, promoted as the 'Rumble in the Jungle'.

Mobutu liked attention and good publicity as it helped bring in the aid money to help him become the world's richest dictator. Shamefully, the West turned a blind eye to this ransacking of his country and the neglect of his people.

As we travelled, we heard that inflation was continuing to rocket, that soldiers hadn't been paid for months, that many of the big ferries on the Zaire River had stopped because there was no money to fix them, and of course, that the roads department had taken their diggers home. Things were not going well for the country and Zaireans were struggling. As a group of white travellers in a fancy-looking truck, we were seen as fair game for a bit of money-making. Who could blame people really, but it meant we had to guard the truck or we had things stolen. So far, we'd lost an outside light, a stool and diesel. We were also constantly surprised and often amused by the ingenious ways people thought up to get money out of us.

'Bonjour. Vos papiers, s'il vous plait,' said the friendly soldier who came to the cab window when three soldiers stopped us on the road one day. I handed our truck papers over.

'Mhm. English?'

I confirmed that most of us were. He gave the documents back. 'Yes, it's good. Passport?' I found it and gave it to him. He looked carefully at the photo and then at me.

'Good.' He returned my passport but still didn't say we could go. They all had guns so you don't try to second guess such guys. 'But—' he continued, 'but where is your triangle?'

'Triangle?' I queried, not understanding.

He smiled, probably confident that we couldn't produce one. 'Triangle for emergency,' he explained, knowing full well that no-one used them and instead used big fallen branches and foliage

146

from the forest edges as vehicles were less likely to drive over those.

'Oh, our warning triangle. Yes, we have one of those. Here you go,' I said, digging it out from behind my seat. You could see his hopes dashed against the door.

'I see. I see. Yes, good.' He thought again. 'And where is your fly spray?'

Ah, he had us. I looked at him and shrugged. 'No, we don't have fly spray, I'm afraid. Is that law?' He smiled more widely this time. He knew he'd got us.

'Oh yes, law. Sure, sure. Law. It is cinq milles zaires for no fly spray. I am sorry.'

We paid the man his 5000 zaires (about £4). He'd won. The smile was worth it.

'Bon voyage,' he shouted, as the soldiers waved us off like old friends. In some countries, corrupt officials or military would use such ill-gotten gains to line their pockets. Not these guys, you could tell. These three were going to eat.

Of course, the dwindling of Zaire's fortunes had little immediate effect on us and our journey other than the scarcity and inflated price of diesel and the state of the roads. In better times, the Zairean roads department would come along every now and then with a huge grader to flatten the worst of the cavernous holes. But there were still far too few graders and far too many miles of road to contend with, so any journey through Zaire in the 1990s was a test of driving skill, patience and nerve. And even a newly graded road didn't necessarily last that long. As soon as the heavy rains came, torrents of water would quickly carve channels and fissures — sometimes deep and wide — in the all-too-temporarily smooth road. When the inevitable happened and one of the huge, overloaded trucks got stuck, the drivers would dig up the road to get themselves out of their predicament, then carry on their merry way leaving a disaster zone behind them which the next truck would get stuck in. And so the cycle continued. In the dry season, these holes and scars were bad enough as they were rock hard and difficult to negotiate, but in the wet season a layer of slippy wet mud turned them into an altogether different kind of treacherous. It was trial by mud.

I found driving on these roads petrifying and exciting in equal measure. It was me versus the road. At the start of a bad patch, my heart would race, but if I got through without sliding sideways into the verge or falling prey to a sudden crater in my way, I was elated. When I misjudged something and we ended up with wheels spinning or bogged, going nowhere, I was disappointed in myself, but the group never seemed bothered because we'd all been led to expect this. Everyone got out and started pushing or putting vegetation or mud mats under the wheels, whatever was needed to get us going again. In the first week, it never seemed to take us too long to get back on the road, maybe up to an hour. I was beginning to wonder what all the fuss was about. It was tough, but it wasn't *that* bad.

CHAPTER EIGHTEEN
A letter from Zairean bog holes

29th October, 1990
A mud hole about 25 kms south of Beni, Zaire

Dear Guy

I'm writing this in Zaire but we haven't got a postal town until Central African Republic. Sorry, it might be a long one!

Well, this is fun! We arrived at this hole at 1 p.m yesterday. Five trucks are stuck blocking our way and we can't get them out. We aren't stuck yet but we just can't get past. So it's now 11 a.m and we all spent the night in the middle of the road in the cook tent with a rain river streaming through it. A Ugandan truck driver let some people sleep in the back of his empty trailer. Looks like we're going to be here for another night. Meanwhile, the bog hole gets boggier, we get muddier and our schedule is blown right up the spout. We are ten days late now. It's raining practically every day and the roads are just a mess. We haven't even got to the supposedly bad ones past Epulu. One truck driver said it would take us weeks to get to Kisangani. 'It is terrible, monsieur.'

It's now 4 p·m· The truck smells a lot like fourteen very ripe camembert cheeses have been hidden somewhere· Oh yes, in the wellies· So far today I've been reading (you should read 'Oranges are not the only fruit' — it's full of good northern humour, but then maybe you wouldn't understand it!), I've practised the guitar (I've decided to avoid 'F' at all costs because it's impossible), made a tape for Mum and Dad, and I'm slowly getting through a rather good bottle of Hennessy brandy· I might even write a book while we're here as I think we'll have time· We're definitely here for another night so I'm preparing a birthday party for Jane tonight· Pete and I took a hair-raising taxi ride back to Beni to get food· What do you reckon to pumpkin soup and chicken cacciatore with garlic potatoes, followed by banana and carrot birthday cake? All swilled down with a brill punch! I think it might go down all right· At least there's a stream to wash in·

3rd November· Another bog hole between Beni and Mount Hoyo
We got out of that last hole after nearly five days· What a bun fight! Buddha the Bastard, in a semi-trailer, faffed around and held everyone up, but we got out thanks to a mega truck-train-tow-chain about eight trucks long· It was brilliant! Everyone around the boghole cheered and danced· Just before we got through, one truck behind us just slid off the road through a seemingly tiny hole in the vegetation and disappeared backwards

150

down the edge of the hillside· The jungley undergrowth just swallowed it· Scary· It could so easily have been us· No-one was hurt and we all helped haul the drivers back up to the road· God knows what they do now·

We've started all night guard duties now because we're getting diesel stolen· It's hard to get here at the moment and this lot cost us $2 a litre on the black market·

The night we spent at a Catholic Mission in Beni we had a tent slashed and Ali's whole backpack was nicked· The next day was tough· Ali came with me and we spent most of the day at the local militia's office· They told us they'd found some kids who'd stolen some pans and things and they beat them in front of us until they told them who'd stolen the backpack· Poor kids· To my shame, we said nothing because it was so scary· Then the militia went and charged into the house of the mother of the thief· Then, because there was no pack there, it all got even worse· In fact, it was horrendous· Ali and I were in a tiny room making a statement (how we wish we'd never reported this) and a woman was brought in· She was apparently the thief's mother· She was standing right next to me with a baby tied to her back· A soldier came in· He looked very intimidating and we just wanted to leave· He told the woman to put her palms together· Then he put three thick sticks between her fingers· Ali and I still hadn't a clue what was going on· He said something to her then he proceeded to squeeze the sticks together on both sides of her hands· I can't imagine the agony that must have been. She screamed louder than anyone I've ever heard before and was reeling but couldn't go anywhere. And then they brought in a boy of about fourteen and did the same to him. I can't tell you how bad we felt, how frightened and shocked we were, and we could do nothing. Or rather, we felt we could do nothing. I so wish I'd had more guts and had been able to tell them to stop. Why didn't I do that? And what gets me is that I guess they can't consider that too bad a punishment as they did it right in front of us 'mzungu' tourists AND there was a crowd of kids outside the office having a good laugh. I couldn't believe it! I'm certainly seeing Africa. We never did get Ali's pack back so we're all sharing clothes with her now.

Yesterday we actually managed fifty kilometres. Amazing! I drove all the way, going through the most unbelievably huge mud holes. One was about three hundred metres long with about a four-metre-deep drop at one point followed by a mega-steep bank. It took a few tries but luckily it hasn't rained for three days now so it was starting to dry out. Eventually we hit the convoy of trucks we were with at our five-day hole — including Buddha the Bastard. It was dark by then but in the gloom we saw a massive five or six-metre-deep hole about a hundred metres long with one or two metres of water in it.

So this morning we've spent two hours bailing the smelly muddy water out and we've just got through it. It took

152

us three hours. We got to go first as the other trucks wanted to use our tow rope. Unfortunately, though, we're now stuck waiting for our rope because the drivers won't give it back. Aaagh!

I am having great fun though. You live for today 'cos you don't know what the next hour will bring, plus it's a real challenge and it's bloody exciting sometimes, especially the driving. Zaire is infuriating yet utterly beautiful. If you can keep calm and stay cheerful in all this, you can do it through anything! Having said that, Freddie has nearly throttled two guys already. He dragged one jeep driver out of his seat because he parked right in front of us at a hole when he said he wouldn't. He moved his vehicle! These mud holes are good for letters though, aren't they? I've never written so much in my life. No dinner for us tonight, just brandy and a game of chess with Joe. We all slept on the truck.

5th November

After a night at River Loya, we thought it would take us about one hour to get to Komanda but one of the two trucks ahead of us slipped off the road. So we put on the chains, got out the tow ropes and went to the rescue. We got out unscathed but it took us until noon to get to Komanda. Then we were off. A decent road at last. It's a bit like being on an earthen Roman road — straight yet undulating — but in a rainforest. It's stunning. At one point it stretched away for miles ahead of us flanked by the never-ending trees and, as always, there were women wearing brightly coloured dresses walking with their kids or men cycling along the road to who knows where· We managed an incredible hundred and twenty kilometres· Amazing· Tonight we're at a protestant mission near Mambassa·

6th November, Epulu

We hit Epulu at last· Only fourteen days late! It's paradise here after so many days of mud· There's green grass, a huge river, 'proper' squat toilets (you just have to ignore the cockroaches), someone to do washing, sun, and equatorial forest everywhere·

After a big truck clean, we went for a wonderful walk in the forest with some Pygmy guides· Our guide showed us trees with roots above the ground, a bat tree, mushrooms we could eat and other plants the Pygmies make into rope, plants for snake bites, and a spiky tree whose spikes can be boiled and drunk with honey for coughs· I found it utterly fascinating· I bought some real bows and arrows from the Pygmies for 2000 zaires (about £1·50)· Oh, and there's an okapi here — you know, the animals that look like a cross between a giraffe and a zebra· They're amazingly rare· It's in captivity, though, which is very sad, as are some chimps here· I did love seeing them but captive animals sit badly with me· John and I were on cook duty tonight so we cooked some skinny chickens with Yorkshire puds, roast spuds and veg, and apple crumble and custard· I greased the truck while dinner was in the camp oven· There were huge flying beetles everywhere tonight· Yuk!

10th November, Kisangani
Yesterday was a shit of a day· I'm still pissed off today· On the 8th, we did an unheard of 230 kilometres so we were all hoping to reach Kisangani late yesterday· It started OK — thirty kilometres in an hour· Then we hit a hole· It didn't look too bad but it had two pipeline lumps in the middle and it was uphill·
I went in as fast as possible but it wasn't enough to get over the lumps and I got stuck between the two· Freddie still sometimes treats me like a rookie trainee and he immediately had his 'we-wouldn't-have-got-stuck-if-I'd-been-driving' face on and started spouting that I should have gone in fast· I had· He made a really big deal about pacing around the truck tutting as if we hadn't been in much worse situations· He spent ages telling me to try and move it backwards by rocking it· The third time, he told me to try again and 'don't bang the clutch this time·' I decided I'd had enough of his tantrum so I said no and that we should go forward and not back· The retort was basically, 'You know stuff-all about it, but go on, waste your time·' So I did· Everyone (except Freddie) helped me pile logs and mud between the holes and then put the mud mats on top· We got out on the first try· Thank God!

So then we went on again and about fifteen kilometres

later we hit another hole· This was just one big steep-in steep-out hole, and dry· I took it slowly in, then, as my front wheels hit the bottom I put on the revs — as Freddie had taught me· We nearly made it· I reversed out and tried again· Still no good· I tried rocking it, no good· So again, I reversed out and tried once more· This time there was a loud snap and the sound of crashing metal· Yes, you guessed it — the springs· It was quite impressive: two helpers and the two springs below them all snapped off on the back right, just after the centre bolt·

Freddie and I got out to look and he just said, 'Four· Well, you've done really well, Amanda·'

I walked straight back to the truck, found my Pygmy bows and arrows, and, as Freddie bent over to inspect the damage, I speared him in the backside·

No, OK, not really· But honestly, I was so mad· For a start, everyone knows that he drives Huwey far harder than me, and this hole wasn't particularly hard on the truck· When I looked, it was obvious that the spring under the helpers had been broken for a while, plus the torsion bar is broken at the moment which probably also strained the springs· All in all, I reckon I was just unlucky to be driving when they went· Freddie doesn't think so, so I'm fuming and ignoring him· In fact, it only took us three hours to change the springs, and today he got us into a tiny hole that has taken us five hours to dig the truck out of because he took it wrong· At least he had the decency to look embarrassed, though he knows better than to talk to me at the moment·

Shortly afterwards, we got to another huge hole with a massive queue of trucks waiting to get through. We were convinced we'd be here for days as one of the guys at the side of the road said no-one had managed to get through for two days. Bum. But then, miracle of miracles, a grader arrived! It took the driver just three hours to flatten the hole enough for us all to get through. What a hero. We got charged 5000 zaires to get past. Fair enough.

So we're now at the Olympia Hotel in Kisangani. We're halfway through the country. What a helluva day. We got here at about 11 p.m, had a tough steak 'cos we were all starving hungry, and went to bed. I'm still not talking to Freddie.

Wish you were here with me. I'd like a hug.
Night.
All my love xxx

CHAPTER NINETEEN
When I paddled down the Congo ...

The highlight of Kisangani was a tailor's shop where they made clothes out of old flour sacks printed in blue with the words: *Farine de froment de premier choix — Produit de la Republique de Zaire* (Top grade wheat flour — Product of the Republic of Zaire). Guide books claim that the mosque or the Boyoma Falls were the must-see places here, but we were overlanders and these unusual clothes were African overlander chic. We put in our orders on our first morning (about £1.50 for a pair of shorts and £3 for a dress) then sploshed around town in the rain. Our planned truck clean was abandoned as it was raining so hard. That definitely didn't help Freddie's already foul mood. I'd never known him like this as he usually snapped out of any dark moods quite quickly. He and I did the essential maintenance work on the truck but you could cut the atmosphere between us with a knife. I knew he was under a lot of stress and I suppose I should have tried to jolly him out of his gloom but I was still really pissed off with his attitude towards me and I just couldn't get past that.

That evening, at a restaurant in town, Jeremy and Dave started talking about what an amazing adventure it would be to go upriver by ferry boat.

It sounded like a mad idea, but actually . . . Two hours later, with dinner only just arriving, the barmy idea had caught the imagination of a few of the group.

'Oh hell, I'm never coming back here, am I?' said Jeremy Joe. 'Let's do it. Who's coming? It's now or never. Live for the moment and all that, eh? Amanda?'

'Me? I can't, I'm driving, you clot.'

'Go if you want,' muttered Freddie.

'What?'

'Well, it would be safer if one of us went with them, so it makes sense if they want to do it.'

'But what about the drive to Bumba? Can you cope alone?'

'It'll be fine. It should only be four days. You go.'

Freddie and I both knew we needed a break from each other and how thrilling would it be to go by ferry up the river?

'Okay, Joe, yes, count me in, though we'll be very lucky if there even is a ferry.'

Early the next morning, those of us keen on the river trip went down to the dock to see about ferries.

'Ah non. Pas de bateaux, madame. Seulement les pirogues. Là bas.' The man pointed to an area down on the riverbank where dugout canoes of various lengths were lined up.

'He says no ferries, only pirogues,' I translated. 'What do you all reckon? I'm up for it.'

And so our 'famous five' Congo River adventure began: *Jeremy Joe, Andrea, Jan, Dave and Amanda paddle down the Congo from Kisangani to Bumba.*

In our truck, Huwey, we were already off-grid — not even Dragoman HQ knew exactly where we were — but on the river we'd be heading even deeper into inaccessible parts of Africa.

159

There were hundreds of miles of fast-flowing water lined by thickly forested riverbanks for us to get lost in. If our adventure became a misadventure, the chances of finding us would be slim. We'd just be a sad headline in one of the back pages of the world press: Five Travellers Disappear In Central Africa.

Obviously, setting off on a four-day journey in a wooden dugout canoe in the middle of one of Africa's most remote regions is the kind of expedition that requires a lot of meticulous planning. We'd need the best guides, a pirogue we could trust, back-up, provisions and gear, maps, and plans of where we were going to sleep each night.

And so it was that a full hour later, we raced back to the truck having hired a large pirogue and two guides in the shape of an amiable young Zairean called Demol and his silent friend we eventually named Fred, who assured us that the journey to Bumba would be 'pas de problème'.

After lunch, the rest of the group left us on the riverbank with three tents, a camp stool each, a small gas stove and a couple of pans, plates and mugs, some basic provisions including rice, tea, canned food and fresh water, a small first aid kit and a few belongings each.

'See you in Bumba on the sixteenth!'

We waved off Huwey and our friends and headed down to our pirogue. Our home for the next four days was about six metres of hollowed-out tree trunk just wide enough for one person. We piled all our gear in the middle and wrapped it in plastic sheeting against the rain we would inevitably come across at some point. There was no shelter for us though, we'd just have to get a soaking if the weather turned against us. Demol and Fred came and went organising goodness knows what until three hours somehow passed and it was just after four o'clock when we eventually pushed off from the shore, bang on time, by local standards, for our one o'clock departure.

We had just two hours until nightfall, we were sitting in a large log, we didn't really know if Demol knew where he was going or how long it would take, and we had no idea where we would be sleeping tonight.

'Look at that,' said Jeremy Joe, poking me in the back. He pointed to a few rough mounds of grey clay in the bottom of the pirogue. 'Do you think our log is more sieve than boat?'

'Ach, it's fine,' I said. 'After bailing out all those bogholes I reckon we're pretty shit hot bailers now, don't you? We can use our cereal bowls!'

'Oh, yes, that's all right then,' he said, airily.

Oddly, there was no sarcasm in his reply. He meant it. There's no doubt that we were all taking a massive leap of faith on this trip, but we just knew it was all going to be okay. If you're like me and your image of African rivers is taken from too many Saturday morning TV films like *Tarzan's Greatest Adventure*, a trip on the Zaire River could initially be a bit of a letdown. For a start, in my opinion it sounded better when it was called the Congo River. 'When I paddled down the Congo' sounds much more exciting and mysterious than 'when I pirogued down the Zaire'. Happily, the name did revert to the Congo River after Mobutu Sese Seko's despotic reign ended in 1997 and the country became the Democratic Republic of Congo. Apart from the name, though, we found there was a disappointing lack of twisty, narrow stretches of water in the midst of rampant overgrown jungle. There was no hacking our way through lianas and old man's beard, and the Guinness-brown waters were not seething with crocodiles just waiting for a careless hand to trail the surface, though I admit to being rather thankful about this last point. No, the Zaire, now Congo, is wide, so wide in places that it's more like a sea. At its broadest point, it's reckoned to be about ten miles across though its main course is broken up into narrower channels — which still seem immense — by countless sandbanks and islands. It is recognised as the world's deepest river and it is Africa's second-longest river after the Nile. This is a seriously impressive river and we were about to paddle along two hundred and fifty miles of it.

About half an hour after setting off, we stopped at a small siding where three men were selling, amongst other things, paddles. Despite being everyday work objects, they had nevertheless been lovingly fashioned and carved.

'Combien pour cette pagaie?' I asked, picking out a tall paddle with a plain shaft and a simply carved blade.

The sellers were rightly proud of their work and felt that they should ask for an exorbitant fee from these rich *mzungus*. And so it was that I became the proud owner of a beautiful six-foot high paddle (a good stretch taller than me) for the ridiculous price of . . . fifty pence. It was a happy transaction. I'd never owned a Zairois paddle before and, according to Demol, the craftsman I bought it from was off to celebrate his sale with a skinful of banana beer. Jeremy Joe and Jan also bought paddles so it looked like we were set to be a bit of a racing pirogue. Four days from Kisangani to Bumba? Pah!

It wasn't long before daylight began to fade and soon we were paddling along in the pitch black. Fireflies started their nightly dance on the riverbanks and further into the secret blackness of the jungle, cicadas were broadcasting their high-pitched throbbing song which is such an innate part of life in the forest. The occasional whoops of monkeys echoed down the river and the blood-curdling screams of tree hyraxes — a small nocturnal furry animal whose nearest relative is, surprisingly, the elephant — sent shivers down our spines. This was the untouched Africa we'd been hoping for. The safety and familiarity of our truck had gone and we were adrift from everything we knew. The night sky held no respect for our paltry torches, the wild river swept us along forcefully to wherever it was going, and the ebony forest discouraged all curiosity, at least until dawn.

It had been a cloudy afternoon and we soon found ourselves in the calm centre of three separate storms. Sheet lightning emphasized the dense clouds high above, and the darkness was fractured by jagged silver spikes that stabbed at the passive rainforest. The heavens were certainly putting on a spectacular first night show for us and we watched in awed silence as the dramatic storms raged around us and distant thunder rolled towards us like the faraway applause of a stadium audience. Adrift in untamed nature, we were as defenceless and insignificant as a leaf floating on the water. It was simultaneously thrilling and humbling. We'd taken a risk coming on this river journey, chasing an adventure that would certainly challenge us but which we also hoped would bring us excitement and a sense of achievement. At that moment in the electrifying blackness, I think we all felt rather vulnerable but also intensely alive. I was more present in the moment than I think I have ever been.

Soon our guides headed towards a patch of cleared forest where we could make out the light of a fire and a small group of huts. Demol clambered up the bank and disappeared to ask the family if we could stay with them for the night. He returned with a tall, wiry man wearing tattered brown trousers and a maroon tank top. Judging from the huge smile on the man's face we were most welcome, and we started to offload our gear from the pirogue into eager helping hands. It seemed that we were the guests of the chief and were welcome to pitch our tents and cook our evening meal in his backyard. We'd been in Zaire for about three weeks now but in some ways this felt like our first night in the dark heart of Africa. We were at the mercy of guides we didn't know from Adam; we were travelling in a leaky log; we'd invited ourselves to be guests of a random family who lived in the forest; and no-one, including us, knew where we were. Yet that night we slept without a care in the world just trusting we were safe.

About five o'clock the next morning, we were awoken by giggling and squeaking, as the family's children tried to peer through the mozzie netting of our tents. We spent a heart-warming hour or so making tea and eating fruit while playing with the kids and talking to the family with Demol as our interpreter. We gave them small gifts as a thank you for hosting us for the night and left with hugs from the mama and warm handshakes from the chief. They waved us off as if we were firm friends.

It didn't take us long to get into the rhythm of life on the river. We took turns paddling and when we weren't doing that we would read, take photos or write diaries. Sometimes we chatted non-stop, telling each other stories and making each other laugh, but at other times we didn't speak for ages, we just looked. We did a lot of looking; looking and daydreaming, and we also waved from morning to night. We waved at excitable naked children in tiny canoes, families on their way to goodness knows where, long dugouts full of people singing as they went along, passengers in jam-packed pirogue-taxis floating by like colourful Picasso paintings, and every now and then we waved at people on huge freight barges pushed by tugboats. These freight boats were usually carrying not just diverse cargo but also hoards of people who had camped out wherever they could find a spot to wedge themselves into, along with their pigs, goats, chickens, monkeys . . . they were like floating shanty towns, often with small pirogues temporarily attached to them like cleaner fish as locals came to trade goods and services.

When we passed huts, the adults raised a hand and smiled in greeting and the kids got super-excited and screamed and waved at us. They ran along the riverbanks until they could go no further, then threw themselves in the river and swam towards us. Sometimes we stopped to say hello but mostly Demol encouraged us to keep paddling.

'It is long. We must paddle.'

And so paddle we did, from about five or six in the morning for about twelve hours each day. To keep us going we bought carp from fishermen who came up to us to sell their catch, and stopped at riverbank stalls to buy snacks such as nuts, fruit, and fried beignets which were a kind of doughnut fried in environmentally disastrous palm oil.

'Try one of these,' said Demol. As if sharing a bag of sweets, he handed me a small packet made of a large leaf. Inside were disgusting fat grubs about five centimetres long.

''Ugh! No, sorry, I couldn't.'

Dave manned up and took one for the team.

'Bloody hell,' he said. 'That is honestly as bad as it looks.' His eyes started watering.

'Chew it, then,' suggested Jeremy Joe, helpfully. 'You haven't munched him up yet. It would be rude not to.'

'They are good food,' said Demol, laughing at our reactions as he bit into one of the grubs. 'Delicious!'

On the third evening, we stayed with a gorgeous family who entertained us by singing and drumming on an old plastic palm oil container. Carol had a recorder with her and taped them singing then played it back to them. They laughed hysterically then made her play it again and again. We tried to reciprocate by singing something but frankly it was just embarrassing in comparison to the beautiful sounds they made.

By the next morning, I'd developed a pretty impressive headache, probably due to all the unexpected sunshine we'd had each day. I'd have loved to just lie in the bottom of our leaky canoe and sleep but there was no chance. We were supposed to be arriving in Bumba tomorrow but Demol told us that morning that we probably wouldn't make it. I began to worry that maybe Demol was way off on his estimate of how long the journey would take. Freddie and the rest of the group would be anxious if we didn't turn up and God only knows what that would do to Freddie's mood. He'd be mad as hell with me if we made the trip even later. There was nothing we could do except keep on keeping on.

Later that day, as we stopped for a tasty riverside lunch of hot fried fish and grilled manioc, we noticed roiling grey clouds were beginning to blot out the blue sky and sure enough, soon after we set off, fat raindrops started to pelt down in bucket loads. It was surprising how quickly we became chilly if we weren't paddling. The rain thoroughly drenched us, of course, but it also put a dampener on our spirits. Things became even worse that night when Demol suggested we camp at a factory he knew of. It turned out to be a palm oil factory. After days of wild river, pristine forest, tiny huts and pirogues, this sad piece of land denuded of trees and with a huge ugly building seemed totally out of place. And it wasn't just the forest that had been devastated by the factory. The river was polluted and gunged up with orange palm oil. It floated on the water in globs and fatty islands which we had to paddle through on the small tributary off the main river to reach our stopping place. There wasn't a soul around. We camped in what seemed to be a market and we were so tired and so miserable about the place that we didn't even want to get out our tents or cook dinner here. We each took one of the covered wooden market stalls and simply rolled out our sleeping bags on the tables.

It was a cold, damp, oily and thoroughly depressing night, and it was made worse by a gloomy conversation we had about how this beautiful river had been exploited for centuries. In years gone by, its waters would have been forced to carry the ivory of tens of thousands of murdered elephants as that cargo of death and greed was shipped out of Africa to Europe. It also unwittingly helped the slave merchants with their heinous trade in abuse and misery. And now, as we'd seen every day, it was betraying the forest. Huge ancient trees were being felled in the knowledge that they could be easily transported on the river's mighty waters. The rainforest of the Congo basin was being systematically harvested for financial gain with no thought to the environmental repercussions. And then there were the palm oil plantations and factories— No, enough. I tried to sleep.

We couldn't wait to get away from the factory, so after waking early we collected our gear and quickly repacked the pirogue. There was no breakfast so we set off with empty stomachs.

'C'est toujours loin,' said Demol. 'Long way to Bumba.'

'Okay,' I said. 'But can we make it if we paddle hard?'

'Possible, mais difficile.' He didn't sound too hopeful and in fact, I eventually drew it out of him that we had absolutely zero chance of reaching Bumba that day. Bugger.

Our morning might have started badly but it ended up being a fabulous day despite us now being late for our rendezvous with Huwey. The sun returned, we quickly found some food for breakfast and Demol stopped at a good place for us to have a wash and a swim. Apart from the swim stop and food breaks, we paddled hard all day from six in the morning to six in the evening. As the sun nestled itself into the arms of the forest, Demol made up for the dreadful previous night by finding us an excellent dinner of fried plantains, fish and manioc greens, and also another wonderful family who took us in and took us to their hearts for the night.

Each night, we found it so easy to be with the warm, welcoming people who lived on the banks of the Zaire. Spending time with them was a joy and showed us all that however much you believe you might be different from someone who wears ragged clothes and lives in a mud hut on the banks of a remote stretch of river in the middle of Africa, you're not. Their lives might seem mysterious to those of us living city lives or coming from western countries, but barriers are there to be broken. When you spend a night singing, dancing and laughing with people you've just met, you realise that there are far more similarities than differences and that most people in the world are generous warm-hearted people who simply want to lead a happy life in harmony with those around them — wherever they come from. Though I will never know who they were, I will always be grateful to each of these families who looked after us on this journey.

The next morning, we knew we simply *had* to get to Bumba. We decided to leave at five o'clock. Demol reckoned we should reach Bumba by about four in the afternoon.

We took turns paddling for thirty minutes then taking fifteen minutes break. We planned to do this all day. Surely that would give us a fighting chance? After five hours, we stopped at a hut that Demol reckoned might be selling something tasty. Our spirits rose when we discovered the lady of the house was offering pineapples and *kwanga*, a type of soggy, fermented cassava bread wrapped in banana leaves. *Kwanga* was not a taste sensation — in fact it tasted of nothing as it was meant to be dipped in stew or soup — but anything, literally anything, was better than eating those big fat grubs that Demol and Fred loved so much and which was the only other option. Fortified by a short stop and some stodgy carbs, we picked up our paddles and headed off once more.

Half an hour paddling. Fifteen minutes' rest. Half an hour paddling. Fifteen minutes' rest. Four o'clock came and went but Bumba was nowhere to be seen. Five o'clock, six o'clock, seven o'clock, eight o'clock . . .

'Demol, are we were nearly there?'

We were paddling zombies, hardly able to ripple the water let alone move us forward much. The current, Demol and Fred were doing most of the work now. We'd given up standing to paddle as our legs were giving way.

'Maybe one hour, maybe two.'

It was eleven o'clock at night when the sleepless river eventually delivered us into Bumba. We felt a strange mix of relief to have arrived and be allowed to stop paddling, and disappointment to have come to the end of our river adventure.

We'd paddled almost non-stop for about eighteen hours and we were utterly spent. Demol asked around to discover where Huwey and the group were, then sent a boy to tell Freddie we'd arrived. We were unpacking the pirogue when Freddie, Ali, Nicky and a few others came to meet us. I wondered if they'd had a bad time on the roads and what kind of mood Freddie would be in.

'Hey, Amanda. Hey, guys. You made it. Thank God, we were beginning to worry. We thought you'd be here before us but we got in last night.'

We each grabbed some gear and began to walk back to the truck. Freddie came and walked beside me.

'I need to say . . . erm, I was out of order last week. I'm really sorry, I shouldn't have spoken to you like I did in that mud hole. Forgive me?' He gave me one of his goofy grins and I put down my bag and gave him a big hug. I was so pleased and relieved. It was good to see him.

'Of course. Thanks Freddie. I appreciate that. And I'm sorry I abandoned you!'

'You didn't. Right,' he said, 'come on, let's get this lot put away because we're all at a party at a local bar. Lots of Primus beers to drink, and we need to swap stories about the last few days while I'm still awake! I hope your journey was better than ours. We've had a shit of a time.'

Party? Now? Oh hell, why not? You only live once.

CHAPTER TWENTY
Voodoo and nuns

For another seven long dirty days, we glooped through bogholes and traversed treacherous bridges which you'd have thought twice about walking over let alone driving a sixteen-ton truck across. But eventually, thirty-five days after entering Zaire, we inched Huwey onto a tiny ferry with a hand's width to spare at each side. We crossed the Ubangi River into the Central African Republic and headed for the capital, Bangui.

I didn't like Bangui. It was the first city I'd come across where I didn't feel safe. It didn't matter much, though, because Freddie and I had to work flat out during our two days there to give Huwey the TLC he desperately needed to get us home. He'd taken a major battering over the past five weeks and was slowly dying on us. The brakes were so full of mud we could hardly stop, so many rivets had popped out of the bodywork both inside and out that it was surprising we were still hanging together, our starter motor was knackered, the lights on the dashboard kept fusing, the windscreen wipers had given up the ghost, and we were crabbing down the road because our left front wheel was tilting inwards.

Freddie and I slogged away for long hours together sharing tasks that would have had me on the verge of tears back when I started in the workshop but which were now just part of what I did for a living. The only time we took off was to telex Dragoman HQ to let them know we were all right and to visit the post office in the hope of letters from loved ones. I was ecstatic to get letters from Mum and Dad and Guy. The news from Guy was about six weeks old but the unavoidable time lag in our communications somehow didn't matter.

Pakistan, 19th October 1990

Dear Amanda

Jambo rafiki!

I've just been up the Karakorum Highway in northern Pakistan – the old Silk Route that goes across the Himalayas to China. Fantastic scenery and we spent a day up at Hunza and walked to the Uttar Glacier. I've never seen a glacier before. It's a black glacier and it looks like a great scar on mother Earth, oozing black blood. It's fucking freezing. Tomorrow we get to Lahore – it should be hot there. Take me to a desert!

I phoned my folks a couple of weeks ago. Thanks for taking the bubbly to them in Nairobi. They said you seemed to be having a good time, and also that you'd sent a letter to me in Esfahan. I nearly spat. I couldn't believe you'd be so stupid as to write to me in a country Brits can't get into. I was furious for about a week – until I got to Quetta having flown over Iran, got to the truck, and found that Yve had picked up the letter for me which you had addressed to her. I had to take it all back. Of course you weren't that stupid! So thanks for the letter. The rafting sounds exhilarating. I suspect, though, that it is potentially cold and wet and therefore not a sport for me·

I completely get what you said about Africa and being happy· I felt like that when I was there· The place has haunted me for seven years· That's why I'm on the road again and why I'll go back and keep going back· It'll be interesting to see if I get the same feeling in India·

Don't ever stop yourself singing, dancing, smiling, writing poetry and sketching· It doesn't matter if people think you've "gone happy"· That's what life is all about· Give yourself over to pleasure and live by it· Live your dreams and make them happen· I wish I was with you to share it· Lots and lots of love· Take care,

Guy xxx

PS: I'll be posting this in Lahore· Will there be anything from you at the poste restante there? I'm hoping so·

As we drove from Central Africa to Cameroon and on into Nigeria, we left behind the forest greens, russety browns and watery blues of Equatorial Africa. The clouds lifted, the sun shone, the roads were more or less drivable, and we ate dust rather than mud each day.

Our route through West Africa was meant to take us from northern Nigeria down to Lagos, through the skinny countries of Benin and Togo into Ghana, then on to Ivory Coast and up to Mali. Unfortunately, we were still two weeks behind schedule so we had no choice but to sacrifice our visit to Ivory Coast, and a Tuareg rebellion in Mali meant that neither would we be going to Timbuktu.

Leaving Lagos, we skirted along the Gulf of Guinea, a

beautiful stretch of coconut palm-fringed Africa. As a visitor, you could easily limit your view of this coastline to it being a fabulous spot for a beach holiday. You'd certainly not be wrong, but you would definitely be missing out. This corner of Africa is a treasure trove of fascinating history and unique cultures and traditions.

Benin is the birthplace of voodoo. Combining elements of animism and spiritism, it is recognised as an official religion here. Forget the Hollywood-promoted myth of voodoo witch doctors sticking pins into dolls. Like most religions, voodoo aims to do good. It's actually more correctly described as a way of life, one in which all of creation is deemed to be divine, nature and ancestors are worshipped, and all things are spirits. Living humans are spirits that can be seen and ancestors are spirits that are unseen though still very much present among the living. Those in the voodoo faith believe that the veil between the spirit worlds can be blurred through rituals and trance dances. Ancestor worship here is deadly serious as the ancestors are called upon and trusted to guide and protect the living. Voodoo was obvious everywhere we went in West Africa but especially throughout Benin and Togo. In markets, we perused stalls selling voodoo fetishes: shrunken monkey heads, dried lizard skins, desiccated chameleons and all manner of plants, rocks, teeth, toenails, skulls . . . To our western eyes, it was mostly a grisly collection of dead things but to adherents of voodoo, each item had its own unique signature which, used properly, could promote physical, emotional or spiritual healing. Voodoo practitioners were harvesting the essential spirit of objects dead or alive to benefit themselves or others in some way or to appease or worship their pantheon of gods.

Passing through a small village one day, we were kindly

allowed to remain as fascinated onlookers to a small ceremony as long as we offered alcohol for the spirits. Three middle-aged women wearing white wraps had smeared their face, upper chest and hair in white ash. They seemed overwrought and almost angry, their movements were jerky and uncontrolled and there was a wildness about them. They shouted, half-danced and half-staggered around, seemingly unaware of where they were or who the people were around them. Alcohol was poured on the ground by some of the crowd and everyone talked non-stop. Eventually, the women collapsed with a scream and friends held them and fanned them back to normality. Despite not having a clue what it all meant, it was utterly magnetic to watch. But I was left with a feeling of edginess. The intensity of the spirits' desire to be heard through the women and the reactions of the crowd felt almost threatening. If this was typical of voodoo rituals, they were nothing if not in your face. At least we'd not had to witness a live chicken or sheep being offered to the spirits. Live *animal* sacrifices were still common but, thankfully, we'd come about a hundred years too late for the human sacrifices that once routinely took place here.

It's hard to imagine that until about 1900, human sacrifice was an accepted practice; accepted even by some of the victims. And we're not talking about the odd person every now and then. No, the kings of Dahomey, the powerful rulers of Benin and the surrounding region from about 1600 to 1900, were enthusiastic advocates of ritual murder. If they were ill they were not averse to killing a man to ward off their untimely death. They also thought nothing of slaughtering hundreds of people to commemorate the lives of previous kings. And when they eventually succumbed to the inevitable themselves, hundreds or even thousands of prisoners, plus the kings' wives, were sacrificed to see them safely into the next spirit world.

Living in or near Benin or Togo from the seventeenth to mid-to-late nineteenth centuries could be very bad for your health. Not only could you find yourself becoming a sacrificial victim but this was the Slave Coast. Around two to three million people are thought to have been sold as slaves and transported to the New World from here. In nearby Ghana, once known as the Gold Coast, we visited the fifteenth-century Elmina Castle, one of the main places from which slaves, as well as gold and ivory, were shipped to the Americas from West Africa. It was heart-rending to stand in the dank, dark barrel-vaulted cells where men, women and children were packed in like just another commodity. We were about five thousand miles from Zanzibar but the grim past of this beautiful coastline mirrored that of the paradise Indian Ocean island we'd visited just over three months earlier. We were no closer to comprehending the pitiless hearts of ice of the slavers who traded in the misery of their fellow humans.

In the 1600s, the Tofinu tribe in Benin came up with an ingenious solution for escaping both slave traders and bloodthirsty rulers. They noticed that their Fon tribe pursuers would abandon the chase if they fled onto Lake Nokoue near Cotonou. And so a plan was hatched: the Tofinu built houses on stilts in the middle of the lake. The stilt village exists to this day and is home to around thirty thousand people. It's not an easy life here and, as we discovered on our day trip, it's certainly not a sanitary environment, but the residents are resilient people who continue to thrive against the odds in this village which their ancestors aptly named Ganvie. It means 'We survived.'

Camping on a stunning Ghanaian beach, the group were kicking back and thoroughly enjoying a warm, lazy time with beers, barbies and surf. They'd earned it. They all agreed that someone should travel with me to Accra to get our visas for Burkina Faso. The problem was that they each thought the someone should be someone else.

'So will no-one go with Amanda so she doesn't get mugged carrying all our passports and money?' said Freddie. 'You all know she's prone to being mugged!'

Uncomfortable silence.

'Right, you buggers,' I said, 'don't worry, I'll go by myself and defend your passports with my life. Honestly, anyone would think you were on holiday or something!'

I really couldn't blame them and actually I didn't mind. I quite liked the idea of a couple of days by myself with a good book. I was reading *In Xanadu: A Quest* by William Dalrymple, and I took a pen and paper to write letters. I caught one of the shared grand taxis to Ghana's capital and found myself a cheap, tacky, bright blue and candy pink hotel room from which to make my assault on the embassy, hoping that no-one would try a smash-and-grab for my backpack full of important documents and stash of cash. Perhaps surprisingly, given my track record, I got away with it and returned to the truck two days later with passports and visas. We were off to Niger via two nights in Burkina Faso.

Ouagadougou. Isn't that the best name for a city? It's a word that just feels so good to say. Oua-ga-dou-gou. Freddie, Ali, Jeremy, John and I decided to go out for an evening meal here at a restaurant we'd heard about called L'Eau Vive. Burkina Faso is a former French colony so we certainly hoped for good French cuisine but we were also curious about it being run by Catholic nuns. Dressed in the most respectable attire we could muster from our grubby backpacks, we chose a table in the small courtyard at the rear of the unremarkable-looking building.

'Look,' said John, 'proper clean tablecloths, silver cutlery and nice glasses. Definitely a touch of class. I think we're in for a treat.'

The air of serenity in the little restaurant was a world away from the dusty, frantic streets we'd just walked through. We'd not been in a place with such a European atmosphere since we left Nairobi. The nuns were charming hostesses and waitresses, and we relaxed into an evening of tasty food and good conversation, until, at half-past nine, we noticed all the diners falling silent. Instead of the hum of conversation, the sweet sound of singing began to fill the air, softly at first but getting louder.

'Ave Maria, gratia plena . . .'

The nuns held candles in their hands and sang as they walked to the statue of the Virgin Mary a little way behind us. It was a magical moment. I am not religious but the power of that song, in that setting, unexpected as it was, was moving beyond belief. I thanked the Universe, or God, if you will, for the privileged life I was enjoying when so many around me, both living and ancestral spirits, endured such hardships. Trite, perhaps, but nonetheless heartfelt. I knew I would always remember that moment. And I have.

CHAPTER TWENTY-ONE
Desert Storm

The combat phase of the Gulf War, Operation Desert Storm, began on 16th January 1991. Iraq had invaded Kuwait back in August and, after months of sanctions, negotiations and threats, the world had had enough. Global travel had been affected by the instability in the Middle East for months now and even Guy's trip around India was struggling with a shortage of diesel. But it was when the hostilities began that our little posse of adventurers felt the biggest impact of the war.

'I'm sorry, guys, but I have some bad news,' Freddie told the group on our first night in Niamey, the capital of Niger. We'd been in touch with Dragoman HQ earlier that day. 'I'm afraid Algeria is refusing to let British nationals into the country.'

'No! You're joking.'

'Is that the end of the trip then?'

'No, don't worry,' said Freddie, 'Drago is sending a new driver to carry on with Huwey and most of you, but I'm afraid me, Amanda, Ali and Jeremy Joe can't come with you.'

'Well, that puts paid to my Bulawayo to Basingstoke journey, doesn't it?' said Jeremy, sadly. We were all gutted.

Dragoman organised for a formidable Australian leader called Crofty to fly down and meet us in Agadez in Niger. I'd met Crofty back in the workshop and liked him but I also found him dauntingly efficient and I felt particularly stupid around him. He was nicknamed 'the trainee killer' because so few survived him. The plan was for Crofty to drive Huwey and the rest of the group through Algeria. Meanwhile, we four Brits would find a way to meet the truck at Figuig, a remote Moroccan town on the Algerian border. The UK Foreign Office was advising all British nationals to leave Niger, Algeria and even Morocco, and Crofty reported that Sykes was in anxious mode. Sykes didn't easily get anxious.

It was hugely disappointing to be missing the Saharan crossing, but I was pleased we'd at least made it as far as Agadez. I took a real liking to this odd little town. It is a historic gateway town to the Sahara and land of the Tuaregs. Tuareg means 'free people' and these are indeed a tribe of semi-nomadic people whose lives revolve around the Sahara Desert. They are also known as the 'Blue Men' as they traditionally wear indigo-dyed robes whose colour rubs off onto their skin giving them a dark blue hue. With their flowing robes and often carrying a sword by their side, Tuareg men are quite a sight. Seeing them for the first time, I smiled, remembering the men of Jordan's Desert Patrol with their khaki uniforms, long headdresses and silver daggers — it seemed I had a thing for men in romantic costumes and carrying swords.

The sandy streets of Agadez wiggled their way past mostly single storey, mud-brick buildings. In the centre, the Grand Mosque stood proudly with its impressive ancient minaret, one of the tallest buildings ever made of mud bricks, with wooden posts protruding hedgehog-like from all sides of its narrow, twenty-seven-metre-high pyramid. The whole town had a sepia quality to it, as if time didn't really play by the same rules here as the rest of the world and we'd just gone back a few hundred years. I'm sure the inhabitants wouldn't have agreed, but to me Agadez felt lost or forgotten. It had the gentle moodiness of the Casablanca movie. Cries of the muezzins punctuated the day, strains of Tuareg music floated through the streets, and sand rubbed the rough edges off everything.

We stayed at the Hotel Sahara. Someone had thought long and hard about that name. It was full of weird characters, misfits of all nationalities — English, French, German, Ghanaian and Gambian. It had a brilliant dive of a bar full of prostitutes and people doing shady deals, especially with cars brought down through the desert. Surprisingly, the restaurant, run by a rather attractive Frenchman, was excellent. During our three days in the hotel we saw a couple of knife fights, a woman attacking an old woman beggar with a whip, and a guy fighting with a man on crutches. It was madness — a slice of the kind of life I'd never been confronted with before. I'm not too sure why I wasn't frightened but I wasn't. I was more intrigued and curious about these dramatic goings-on.

People-watching was our favourite pastime here but a visit to a silversmith fed my ever-increasing passion for the traditional crafts of the countries I was travelling through. Mohamed was Inadan, a caste of Tuareg artisans, and his skill with silver and leather had been passed down to him through his male lineage. We watched as he put the finishing touches to a *tanaghilt* or 'cross', the most important piece of jewellery for any Tuareg. He explained that there were twenty-one different Tuareg cross designs, with the Agadez cross being the most famous. The crosses he showed us were made of silver or silver alloy using the lost wax method. They were all versions of the original Agadez design which had a diamond shape with extended points, and above it, a ring. Mostly made as pendants, the crosses didn't reference religion but rather the four corners of the Earth. The cross was symbolic of the 'free' Tuareg having the freedom of the world. Unable to say no to beautiful craftsmanship, and loving ethnic jewellery, I left Mohamed's house with five Tuareg crosses, a set of non-traditional but unique chess pieces, and a pendant made from a 1780 Maria Theresa thaler coin which I felt must be quite rare. Sadly, it turned out not to be as rare as I hoped as when the Empress Marie of Austria died in 1780, that date remained on all thaler coins minted from that date on — even today. Since I was not the only one buying big that day, Mohamed had a good day.

For Freddie, Ali, Jeremy and I, the next day was not a good day. We waved our friends off as they headed for the Sahara Desert, worrying because we'd heard that Algeria might be totally closing its borders. What would happen if they got stuck there? But we could do nothing. We flew back to Niamey and hoped for the best.

Sitting on the roof of Hotel Rivoli in Niamey, Jeremy Joe and I watched the world go by. It was the time of the Harmattan which meant it was almost constantly misty-dusty with a drying wind blowing day and night. On the streets strewn with everyday rubbish, eddying sand and dried dates, men with crippled limbs got along on crutches or crawled on the ground and tried to harass tourists into parting with money. Three white tourists fended them off bravely with breakfast baguettes only to escape into the arms of leather box sellers around the corner. Cigarette touts stood in the path of every oncoming white person ('moins cher, monsieur') then chased them doggedly down the street until patience snapped and cigarettes flew. A camel moseyed along looking like a walking haystack. A man with a mat on his head sauntered past looking very silly, but he didn't appear to care. Women on the street sides with their large bowls of samosas or other tasty home-cooked treats fed the ever-hungry men passing on their way to nowhere, and the keepers of travelling cart shops watched eagerly for any glimmer of enthusiasm for their varied goods.

We had to wait for a couple of days for our flight to Casablanca in Morocco. Ironically, it was going via Algiers. We were annoyed and frustrated. It was such an anti-climax to have to end the trip like this. And more than that, for me, Crofty had told me that Dragoman had been expecting me to lead a southbound trip back to Harare leaving in March, but that was now looking dodgy due to the war. I was pissed off.

'Come on,' said Jeremy. 'We can't mope up here all day. Let's get the others and look round the market.'

He was right. We were still here, we could still explore. It was not the kind of hotel you'd leave money or passports in despite the rooms having locks, so we grabbed our valuables and headed out into the hot Saharan hubbub.

Niamey market was crazy busy. We stayed more or less together so we didn't get lost but at one point I found myself quite a way back from the others as I checked out some fabric. It was then that I felt someone touch my shoulder from behind.

'Eh! Bonjour!'

I turned to face a very large, muscle-bound man in an open shirt with a grubby vest underneath. I just knew. His eyes said it all as he quickly noted the string around my neck that held the travel wallet under my dress.

No. Fucking. Way. Not again. I am *not* having this.

His left hand made a move for my wallet string as his right

hand reached into his shirt. I watched as he started to draw out a large knife. I was furious.

'Fuck OFF, you BASTARD!' I yelled as loudly as I could, at the same time grabbing onto my wallet string and yanking it away from him then running like hell through the market to the others. It all happened in seconds.

Of course, he could have easily held on but I think the speed and vehemence of my reaction took him by surprise. Only when I reached Freddie, Ali and Jeremy did I turn. The man had given up and was walking the other way. My heart was hammering and I started to shake as the adrenalin kicked in. I told the others what had just happened.

'Bloody hell, Amanda, have you got a big arrow and a 'Mug Me' sign above you somewhere?' said Freddie, looking at the air above my head.

'Thanks, I'm fine,' I said, laughing.

And, do you know, I was fine. Rattled, for sure, but actually quite proud of myself. I'd taken control, fought back and refused to be a victim. I felt about six feet tall. I felt strong. I felt confident. In this dusty city on the banks of the Niger River, my inner lion had roared her presence.

CHAPTER TWENTY-TWO
Now what?

The narrow, covered streets of the souk in Marrakech baffle all but the native feet which shuffle along in the dense crowd. It was, therefore, a major coup when four pairs of English feet, which had been trying to keep a relatively low profile all morning, found themselves outside the School of the Quran.

'Dix dirhams,' said the bored gatekeeper.

'Freddie, pay the man,' I said, mischievously.

He knew that Ali and I had been buying shoes, lampshades, coats, tacky earrings, dates, walnut boxes and ceramic dishes all morning.

'Have you both spent up already?'

'Well, we might not be coming back,' said Ali, laughing. 'We couldn't miss a bargain!'

The guide at the Quran School looked a lot like a roast chestnut with the shiny bit peeled off, except he was wearing a djellaba. He introduced us to the inner courtyard with a series of single words accompanied by expansive gestures. The frieze, which ran high up on the four walls and consisted of verses of the Quran ornately carved into solid cedarwood, was brought to life by three words spoken very reverently and very slowly by a very toothless mouth: 'Quran, cedar, Lebanon.'

The pleased and proud chestnut seemed in need of

encouragement before moving on, so we dutifully oohed and aahed and repeated the magical words. Yes, that did the trick and he whisked us off to the next room. 'Mosque, Mecca, Quran,' and the next, 'Quran, bookshelf, cedar, marble.'

Just as we thought we were getting the hang of this game, we were stopped mid-ooh with a dramatic 'Aha!' The guide staggered off in the direction of a staircase saying, 'Follow.' We followed him up the stairs, around the bend, and into a tiny room with a makeshift ladder in the corner. The guide seemed to be enjoying himself as he slowly climbed the ladder cackling. His head disappeared into the hole above and then he looked down at us and laughed hysterically. Thank God, at last that gave us a chance to crack up laughing as we'd been itching to do since the start of the tour. The guide was delighted, came down the steps and said to Freddie, 'Up, up.' Freddie went up, looked at the bare floorboards of the attic room above, came down and everyone fell about again. This happened four times. It was strange how the joke didn't wear thin, but then none of us really knew what we were laughing at.

That game over, the guide shuffled us into another room. A very serious look from the chestnut seemed to suggest that joking was over. He pointed to a wall by a door. It was about two feet wide. He ran his finger along the wall twice, saying, 'Petite chambre.' Then he went through the door into the room whose outer wall we'd been measuring. Totally baffled, we all entered the room one by one and were treated to the spectacle of the chestnut flinging his arms wide open and saying, 'Grande chambre!' and laughing so hard he wheezed. This was definitely the best guided tour any of us had ever had. On we went, room after room, giggling all the way, until we reached a kind of inner tower. He stopped us all, then took Joe around a corner, came back and took Ali around another side of the tower, came back and positioned Freddie and myself — each of us at one of the tower's corners. Then the cry went up, 'Look, look!' We all looked, and broke out laughing yet again as we pointed and waved to each other from different sides of the inward-facing tower.

Even the guide realised that nothing could quite top that hysterical trick, so he led us all back to the exit for a fond farewell and, as a last laugh, stung us for a huge tip.

We had two days in Marrakech and despite the British government advising all nationals to leave Morocco we never met with any hostility. Nor did we as we travelled through the country in grand taxis and public buses to reach the remote Algerian border post where we were meeting the group. It was suggested that I should keep my head covered so my blonde hair wouldn't draw attention. Luckily, I was only assaulted once and that was by the rather ripe body odour of the two Tuareg men I ended up squashed between on our final bus journey through the mountains and desert to Figuig.

Figuig turned out to be an impressive oasis town. It started life around the eleventh century and its terracotta mud-brick houses look as if they grew here rather than being built by human hand. Flanked by mountains and with the great sea of the Saharan Desert lapping at its doors, the large town has seven walled *ksour* or fortified districts each with its own huge date palm oasis watered by an ancient irrigation system. The effect of hundreds of thousands of palms in and around this mainly mud city is really rather beautiful and I was pleased we'd managed to see it, albeit for a very short time. The year we travelled here, it was a busy place due to the border traffic but, sadly for the town's prosperity, that was not to last much longer as the border was closed indefinitely in 1994. No more border-crossing trade in Figuig, just cottage-industry crafts and a lot of dates.

For us, a different border crossing was now beckoning. Due to the Gulf War, we were supposedly in non-friendly territory and we'd been told to get out of Morocco without delay. It was great to meet up with Crofty and our friends once again, but the atmosphere of the trip had now changed and in many ways it felt as if our expedition had ended. In a few speedy days, we reached Ceuta on the Mediterranean coast, caught a ferry across to Algeciras in Spain and drove to Gibraltar.

That was it. We were out of Africa. It was such an unsatisfactory ending to our long adventure together but it couldn't be helped. It felt strange to be in Europe. Freddie was going to drive Huwey home alone but, since we were late, I flew back to the UK with the group. It was all so fast. By the end of January 1991, I was back home in Durham.

Now what?

CHAPTER TWENTY-THREE
Winter break

'I'm not washing those, they're disgusting.'

It's a mum or a grandma thing, isn't it? Or at least it was when I was growing up; the view that you have to wear decent knickers in case you're ever caught in an accident. Strange really, as I can't imagine doctors remarking on the state of your underwear if you've been brought into A&E and need to be undressed. Anyway, the knickers that had travelled the length of Africa with me apparently no longer counted as decent so they had to go.

It was wonderful being back home and seeing Mum and Dad. I revelled in doing nothing and having no responsibility other than walking the dog on the fells and helping Mum with the cooking when she would let me. I curled up with a good book by the fire as winter raged around us and the snow drifted to car-burying heights in the Durham hills. I hadn't realised how tired I was but I slept for twelve hours a night for the first few days. It's only looking back on this time that I can see how difficult it must have been for my parents when I chose to head off for months on end into unknown and potentially dangerous countries. They had no word from me for week after week and when news eventually arrived it was old. But they never once tried to dissuade me from going, never told me they were concerned, and always backed all my decisions in life. Their faith in me allowed me to fly. Having me home safely was a relief for them, though, and Mum showed her love and happiness with hugs, good food and also by buying me new underwear. Sometimes it's the little things that say the most.

In February 1991, the UK was sinking under a heavy weight of depression. The Gulf War raged on horrifically. We were in an ever-deepening recession which led to the worst unemployment for decades. The IRA were still attacking whenever they could, including bombing Downing Street on 7th February. There were fuel shortages, no-one was travelling, and, to top it all, the British Isles were being deep-frozen by prolonged Arctic conditions. Despite the snow, after a couple of weeks at home, it was time to return to Suffolk. The thought of sleeping in the Old Dogger caravan in sub-zero temperatures was less than appealing but I had to get back to help with mending Huwey and to find out what plans Drago had for me. Actually, I'd already spoken to Sykes and George, and it seemed like the southbound Trans-Africa was still on the cards but a delay was being considered.

I walked into the New Dogger to see a huge bunch of red roses on the table.

'Ooh, is it someone's birthday?'

'They arrived today,' said Robbo, who'd kindly picked me up from Ipswich station in Van de Merc. 'They're yours.'

'Really? Who are they from?' I looked in vain for a note or card.

He laughed. 'Well, we all assumed they were from Guy, but perhaps there's something we don't know? And by the way, he's calling you here later tonight because he's reached Delhi, so if they might *not* be from him you perhaps need to be careful what you say!'

It was the first time I'd met Rob, an Australian known as Red Robbo by Dragodom due to his ginger hair. There tended to be no subtlety in the nicknames at Drago. If the Trans-Africa trip went ahead he was going to be my co-driver so I was relieved to have taken an immediate liking to him. He liked a chat, had an easy-going yet naughty sense of humour and an infectious smile, but he also put in the work and, importantly, seemed completely fine about me being his leader on this trip.

'God, I hope Sykes and G let us go,' he said. 'But did you hear about Stevie and Andrew?'

I hadn't.

'Just the other day, they were held up at gunpoint in Algeria. They'd avoided towns as much as they could but they were attacked in the middle of the desert. It sounded bloody scary. Stevie said the men were very angry and shouted right in their faces. He felt the man's spit hitting his cheeks. He was convinced they were all going to die. Stevie and Andrew were forced on their knees and had guns pointed at their heads. The men were wanting to know why Britain and America were bombing Iraq and asked if there were any Brits or Americans on the truck. Obviously Stevie lied and said no, but the bloke slapped him and Andrew about anyway. They just kept their heads down, didn't make eye contact, and pretended not to understand French. The man eventually calmed down and left them. So they were all fine in the end.'

Oh, that's all right then! Jesus, that was absolutely *not* what I wanted to hear. I was immediately taken back to the Burundi-Zaire border post a few months earlier. As I drove up to the gate, I saw the young soldier with his gun. That wasn't unusual but when I reached him, he pointed the rifle straight at my head through the cab window. He was shaking and shouting at me. God knows why he thought we might be dangerous but a jittery soldier with a gun was not a comfortable thing to be faced with.

'Nous sommes des touristes,' I said, trying to smile calmly and showing him my empty hands. 'Pas de problème.'

I think me being a woman made him feel less threatened, so he dropped his gun quite quickly but it was still unnerving, to say the least. Stevie and Andrew's experience was a whole other level of terrifying. Was Sykes really still going to send us through there? I was very much up for the adventure but I didn't fancy putting my life on the line or being taken hostage. I probably wouldn't even be allowed a visa again, so Rob would have to drive through on his own. That didn't sound like a great idea either. Some of the passengers must have been thinking the same about the whole trip, as Rob and I were told that four people had backed out and we were down to thirteen passengers now. Things were not looking great.

However, we carried on fixing up Huwey and making all our preparations at Camp Green as if nothing was wrong. It was all as bonkers as usual at the workshop. G seemed to swing from childishness to attempts at guru-like wisdom. One moment he'd be saying that we had to get the trucky-wucky ready and at the next he'd state sagely that 'I've got this life thing sussed.'

Crofty was also in playful mood and kept attacking me with rivets. I returned fire with oranges. It seemed odd now that I'd found Crofty daunting to be around previously. He was great fun once he'd decided you weren't a shirker or a complete waste of space. It seemed I'd passed the test. We also had a fabulous night of being complete drunken idiots on the occasion of Marty's stag night. Marty was G's brother and he worked the farmlands of Camp Green along with the indomitable Bowler. Together they were known to us as Bowmart; bodgers extraordinaire, no job too small or weird. They weren't part of Dragoman but since the company was based on the farm we saw a great deal of this pair of jokers, piss-takers and all-round lovely people. Life at Dragoman was filled with unforgettable characters, and after nearly three years, many of them were like my second family. This wasn't a job, it was a way of life. At least for now.

On February 28th two wonderful things happened: the Gulf war ended with Iraq retreating from Kuwait, and my sister Sam decided she was coming on the trip with us. The ceasefire was superb news, not only for the obvious reason of stopping yet more lives being tragically lost but also because it meant our Trans-Africa trip was definitely going ahead. Sam's news was completely out of the blue.

'Well, that's great. Isn't it?' said Rob.

'Totally,' I said. 'I'm just in shock. I never thought she'd even dream of coming on an overland trip, let alone a long Trans-Africa. She's never been the adventurous type and I always thought she thought I was mad for doing this.'

'She has a point, of course,' said Rob. 'None of us can really be in exactly sound mind to be doing this as a job, can we? I know I'm not!' He pulled a stupid face.

Sam is three years younger than me. When we were young, she was always the one who liked to play in the mud and was a bit of a tomboy, whereas I hated getting my hands dirty and wanted to be clean and wear nice clothes. How things change! By our mid-teens, we'd pretty well swapped roles. We were both very happy at home and our family was very close, but once I went to university she never thought to come and visit me in Leeds and I never thought to invite her. From that time on, I only saw Sam

193

during the holidays and we rarely spent much time together. She did very well at cookery college and got a job in London as a food and beverages manager at a Heathrow airport hotel. I was so proud of her. However, she lacked self-confidence and when the hotel was going to be taken over by Hilton, she panicked and resigned, certain she would be let go for being a poor manager. This event came at the same time as her boyfriend decided to go to work in Riyadh for a year. She was floundering. A trip to Africa with her big sister seemed like an escape to be grasped.

I was partly delighted and partly anxious about it. She'd never camped before and liked her home comforts; she didn't like dirt; she had bad eczema; she was socially anxious and unsure of herself around people she didn't know; she was quite easily frightened of unknown situations, and I wasn't aware of her having any interest in travelling or Africa. It would be great to share this with her but I hoped this wasn't a decision she'd live to regret.

And so it was that on 10th March 1991, Rob and I set off in dear old Huwey who was looking super smart in his new paintwork though missing Freddie's butcher's awning which G had taken an instant dislike to. We had a small group of fourteen passengers including my sister and, to both her and my surprise, Kathy from my Middle East trip with Guy. It was great to see her again. This expedition wasn't the West African route I'd just finished with Freddie but a slightly shorter version going directly from Morocco to Algeria, Niger to Nigeria, then through Cameroon to Central African Republic and on to Zaire and East Africa. We would reach Zimbabwe in mid-August.

This time it was *my* gig. It was down to me to get these fourteen lovely people through Africa safely whilst giving them an experience of a lifetime. Thankfully, though, I would be sharing the work, responsibility and the fun with Robbo. I was the one with the knowledge of the route through Africa, but Rob wasn't a trainee as he'd already led trips. He knew what the job entailed and his mechanics were much better than mine. I just knew we were going to have a great trip together. I was happy. We were off on another adventure and, more than that, in my pocket I had a letter which had arrived at the workshop just in time.

15th Feb 1991

Dear Amanda
I'm sitting in Delhi campsite and I've lost John, my co-driver, and the truck. John went off five hours ago for diesel and hasn't been seen since!

It was so good to speak to you the other night. You sounded a long way away, probably because you are. You also sounded like you've spent a week or two at home because your accent has come back really strongly.
I was so pissed off (well, not really) that you didn't think the roses were from me. I suppose you've got so many admirers that they could have been from anyone. I just figured I didn't need to send a message because you'd know, know that I need to be with you, share with you and just have you near. I need to speak to you every day, not once every six months and letters every couple of months. What are you doing? Who are you with? Are you happy? Are you missing me? What I'm trying to say is that I'm very much in love with you and think of you all the time. I wish we were together.

I don't think I told you before but do you remember that evening when we were doing the twenty-four-hour drive and we stopped at that awful truck stop for food? You danced around the truck in your yellow summer dress, and you were like a small child dancing, turning, spinning in the evening sun· It was like watching someone free and uninhibited celebrating life· Did you know everyone was watching you? You certainly danced as if no-one else was there· Well, that night, I saw your soul· It danced too· It danced with you and around you, it danced in perfect freedom· And it danced over to me, reached out and touched my soul· It was at that precise moment that I fell in love with you·

*I hope you're not so knackered as to have harmed that free spirit· But then, I don't think anything could·
Have fun, take care,
Lots and lots of love
Guy xx*

CHAPTER TWENTY-FOUR
Until . . . nothing

By the time we left Paris, we were running five days behind schedule. I could hardly believe it. My nemesis, the Central African Republic visa, had reared its ugly head once again and, after being given the run around for a few days, we had to admit defeat and trust the ambassador's promise that Rabat in Morocco would be able to issue the visas for us. I hoped to God he wasn't just saying that to get rid of us.

'We're not going to Rabat, are we?' said Rob.

'We are now. We can't wait around in France any longer, we'll have a mutiny on our hands.'

Thankfully, Rabat came up trumps and, at last, we could head for Marrakech and the group could start to enjoy the journey we were meant to be having instead of just pottering around Europe and enduring the faffing about of annoying embassy officialdom.

Marrakech felt like the real start of our expedition. Despite the rather fraught circumstances of my last visit, I'd fallen hook, line and sinker for this beautiful and ancient walled city. In fact, I decided I'd be very happy to live here. Losing yourself in its labyrinthine souks, you move through covered alleyways crammed with people and lined with shops stuffed with carpets and copper lanterns, decorative pottery, rainbow displays of leather babouches, and multi-coloured pyramids of spices, olives and dates. In the medina, horse-drawn caleches transport people around town, and in the 1990s donkeys and carts were still the go-to equivalent of our white vans. Walking through the streets of each quarter, you find busy mosques and well-frequented hammams, and in the mornings the irresistible smell of freshly-baked bread emanates from the communal bread ovens. I ended up buying bagfuls of herbs and *ras el hanout*, meaning 'head of the shop', which is a concoction of ten or even twenty or more spices which each stallholder views as his very best blend and taste sensation. It really can make the blandest of meals into something quite impressive. Even in winter, Marrakech has a dusky pink glow which gives it a slight air of make-believe. This aura of fantasy becomes even more noticeable as the sun begins to set, especially if you're in the medina's main square, the Djemma el Fna. The Djemma throngs with both local people and tourists all day long. Orange juice stalls and date stalls vie for your business alongside shoe-shine men and fortune-tellers, and water-sellers wearing their traditional garb and bedecked with brass cups and goatskin water bags harry everyone they can waylay, not to drink their water — few are brave or foolish enough — but to have their photographs taken with them, for a suitably extortionate fee, of course. Around four o'clock each day, though, a transformation starts to happen. From hidden alleyways and nearby nooks and crannies, people begin to arrive pushing carts laden with wooden structures, tarpaulins and lights, and in seemingly no time at all, half of the square becomes an outdoor restaurant made up of stall after stall of individual purveyors of mostly traditional Moroccan cuisine. This was an experience we had to savour. Sitting on rough wooden benches in the freezing cold, we ate the most delicious mutton and date tagine or vegetable couscous. Around us, muezzins called the faithful to prayer and we watched as a steady stream of men wearing thick pointy-hooded djellabas filed into the nearby mosque. As the evening wore on and the square got even busier, we noticed clusters of people dotted around. The entertainers had arrived. Cross-legged storytellers had locals enrapt, acrobats got loud cheers, and snake charmers beguiled their audience. We revelled in the fact that all our senses told us that we were in another world; this was not our 'normal'. Our journey to explore Africa had begun and everyone was buzzing.

When we got back to our hotel that night, Rob turned up at my room with a bottle of cold bubbly, a bottle of red wine and two glasses.

'To toast the real start of our trip,' he said.

Now that's the kind of co-driver you need!

We were already giggly after the bottle of bubbly. It was like having a daft sleepover night with a best friend. We laughed like drains and let go of all the tension of the first two weeks of the trip.

'I've got a great idea,' said Rob, around midnight. 'We should play an April fool on Crofty tomorrow before we go.'

'Brilliant!' I agreed. 'What?'

Crofty had taken on an operations role in Dragoman and before we left the UK he told us he was concerned about losing a lot of drivers at the moment. Mr Clean was going to get married, Fi was going to live in Uganda, Jan and Lutey were both retiring.

'How about I tell him I've had enough and I'm leaving in Nairobi?' said Rob.

'Too wicked,' I said, then we fell about laughing at our dastardly plan.

Hindsight is a wonderful thing and we shouldn't have done it, but I suppose a lot of things seem funny after a couple of bottles of wine. Why it still seemed like a good idea the following morning, I have no idea, but our lack of judgement came back to bite us a few weeks later when we found out that Crofty had taken on a new trainee to meet me in Kenya. He was apoplectic when Rob told him he'd been joking. I didn't blame him, we'd been idiots — but it was a very funny evening!

Other than a bit of a meltdown when she met her first cockroach in a shower, Sam seemed to be coping well with the camping and our rather basic Marrakech hotel. I didn't know if she'd expected me to be able to spend a lot of time with her but, thankfully, she quickly realised how full-on my role was and didn't make any assumptions. She also offered to do my clothes washing to take some of my load off. Bless her. I didn't argue. I was relieved to see she'd clicked with her tent partner, a young English doctor called Maddy, and she was getting on well with most of our group of eight Brits, four Australians, three Kiwis and a Canadian. It turned out to be a really fun group and everyone quickly gelled with each other. They were always up for beers and a laugh around the campfire and needed little to no excuse for a party. Morocco was going brilliantly until . . . Why did there always have to be an 'until'? But then, life is full of things going right until they go wrong and, happily, going wrong until they go right.

This particular 'until' occurred in Fez. We had to backtrack to see this famous medieval city since we'd missed it earlier because of going to Rabat for the visas. We knew Huwey wasn't feeling well, and sure enough, when Rob and I checked the engine in Fez campsite, he'd blown a piston ring. Actually, though, the timing was a blessing in disguise even though it didn't feel like it at the time. Another Dragoman truck driven by two friends, Hoggy and Jimbo, was also in Fez on their way back to the UK.

'Just swap the engines round,' said G, calmly, when we rang him. 'Hoggy and Jim will get home no worries, and their engine is still sound so you'll be fine with theirs.'

We hired a truck with gear to lift the engines in and out, and Hoggy, Jimbo, Robbo and I all worked flat out to get both engines swapped and running smoothly. We were already on the drag, of course, and now our three nights in Fez turned into five nights. Being a few days late when you're near the start of a five-month-long expedition is not generally a big deal but I was now faced with a different issue: the Algerian visas of the Aussies and Kiwis in the group were going to run out before we would make it to the border with Niger. Perfect. Yet another obstacle to navigate. I wasn't sure how we were going to fix that little problem but I decided we would head into Algeria anyway and try to organise visa extensions in Tamanrasset, the biggest town we were passing on the way.

For the nine days it took us to get through Algeria from the border town of Figuig to Agadez in Niger, Rob and I were totally reliant on the route notes from previous drivers. I was so excited to be heading through the Sahara Desert at last, and now that the Gulf War hostilities were not throwing a shadow over our journey, I didn't have any sense of fear for our safety.

The Sahara is not an endless sea of golden sand dunes. Certainly the dunes are an extensive and beautiful part of the Algerian Sahara, but there are also vast stretches of barren mountains and sandstone plateaus scored by deep gorges and valleys. Where oases and rivers have enabled lives to be lived and food to be grown, settlements both large and small have grown up over the centuries. Taghit and Timimoun are two such oasis towns. These captivating places are both flanked by mischievous mountains of sand that look solid and immovable but whose fringes dance and fly as they play with the Saharan winds and whose colours change chameleon-like from sharp yellows to burnt umbers and coppery pinks depending on the time of the day and the caprice of the skies. Taghit is a ribbon of greenery squeezed in between the Grand Erg Occidental — Algeria's second-largest stretch of sand dunes — and huge rocky mountains hiding ancient rock art. In Timimoun, red mud-brick buildings are delightfully offset by thousands of palm trees.

These towns reminded me of *Le Petit Prince*, the novella by French aviator and writer, Antoine de Saint-Exupéry. In it, the little prince from another planet says, "I have always loved the desert. One sits down on a desert sand dune, sees nothing, hears nothing. Yet through the silence something throbs, and gleams." He was right. As impossible as it seems, dunes hum with life and magic, and it feels as if the whispering sands would share ancient secrets if you could just tune in to a long lost frequency.

It would have been lovely to spend more time in these small towns but we had to spend four nights in the larger town of Tamanrasset. Once upon a time, this Tuareg stronghold was a French military outpost whose soldiers guarded the trans-Saharan camel caravans carrying salt and other products across these inhospitable lands. It is also the gateway town to the Hoggar Mountains but, sadly, we didn't have time to explore. Instead, I had to endure very unsubtle overtures from the chief of police who took it upon himself to help me chivvy the authorities into parting with visa extensions. Yes, I could have asked Rob to do the running but I think we both knew that the chief didn't fancy him so we were less likely to get what we wanted in any timely fashion.

'Ah, another broken heart left in your wake, Amanda,' said Rob, grinning, as we drove out of town, visas in hand.

'Broken heart my backside. Lecherous sod. My left knee has never had so much attention.'

There was a point on the piste from Tamanrasset to Niger where I decided to stop the truck. Nearly everyone was snoozing, lulled by the noise of the wheels skimming the constant corrugations of sand. We'd been bogged a couple of times already, not seriously but enough to get everyone out and using the sand mats. They all assumed we'd got stuck again, so roused themselves for another session of digging and pushing.

'No, wait,' I said to them all. 'I just thought you'd like to see something. Look.'

They looked.

'I can't see anything,' someone said. 'What are we looking at?'

'Nothing,' I said. 'Absolutely nothing.'

For 360 degrees, there was indeed nothing to be seen. Not a wrinkle of distant mountains nor even a decent-sized rock, no sand dunes or dust swirls, no camels or deep tracks, not even a cloud in the sky. There was nothing. Just us. I don't know if this is unique but surely there can't be many places in the world where from horizon to horizon there is no obvious feature. It wasn't photogenic so I imagine none of us have a photograph of that moment, but I'd like to bet that nearly everyone on the truck remembers that little spot in the Sahara where they saw absolutely nothing.

CHAPTER TWENTY-FIVE
Medicine and magic

'Is anyone else feeling horribly grotty?'

We were in Niamey, scene of my triumph over the last person who tried to mug me (just saying). Two of the group were ill in bed and all they could stomach was rehydration powders. Kathy and Maddy were looking after them but they really didn't look good and said they felt like death. A few hands went up in answer to my question and I had to admit I wasn't feeling too shit hot either. I'd put it down to a recurrence of my giardia but it wasn't quite the same. Despite our best efforts as regards hygiene on the truck, there was no doubt that some unseen nastiness was attacking us.

'I think it was an ice cream that did for us,' said Kathy. 'Anna and Paul just admitted to having one in Tamanrasset.'

'Oh bloody hell, why don't people listen?!' I said.

We disinfected everything we could inside Huwey and I told everyone to be even more careful than normal. However, by the time we reached Kano in northern Nigeria three days later, almost the whole group was down with a bafflingly diverse range of complaints varying from headaches to fever and stomach pains to constipation or diarrhoea. Everyone was extremely cranky and the intense heat made things worse.

This was not normal, not even for overlanders who could

almost rely on getting some form of the trots or some other illness at least once on a trip. I discussed it with Maddy and Rob and we agreed that we should get everyone tested. I found a private clinic and all sixteen of us trooped in for blood and stool tests. Some people were really quite sick, others were just off colour. The only person who was completely healthy was Adrian, the poor English guy who had just joined us in Kano and who was probably wishing he hadn't bothered.

It quickly transpired that every single one of us was properly ill. Typhoid was said to be the culprit so, given the seriousness of that disease, I was hugely relieved we'd decided to get medical help instead of just accepting this as a travellers' bug. Three of us also tested positive for malaria — including me.

'You must stay in hospital,' said the doctor. 'You need antibiotics and fluids urgently.'

'What? All of us? Can't we just get drugs to take away with us?' I asked, not relishing the idea of a hospital stay and having a terrifying phobia of needles.

'It would not be best. Best is that you receive IV medication for a few days and we can ensure you are healthy before you continue your journey.'

Maddy backed up the doctor's insistence on quick intensive treatment, so I gave in. I handed over custody of Huwey to Adrian despite this being only his fourth day in Africa. I fixed him up with a good local guide called Mohammed, a lovely gentle man who spoke very precise English other than the fact that he couldn't say the letter 'f' so for him 'fifty' was 'pipty'.

'Er, actually, Adrian, there is just one other thing,' I said, before we left the campsite for the private hospital. 'Apparently they don't feed us in hospital. We're taking cereal, bread, peanut butter and some other bits with us, but is there any chance you can visit us tomorrow and maybe bring us some more food? I'm so sorry about this. I know it's not a great start to your trip.'

The next three days were rather surreal and disheartening. We were all attached to drips on mobile stands so we could move around the ward to chat with each other, but mostly we lay down, slept and read books or wrote letters. I could imagine Sam's letter to Mum and Dad and cringed to think of their panic when they read: *We're in hospital in Nigeria and we've all got typhoid and Amanda has got malaria too. I'm feeling awful, but I'm sure I'll be fine.*

I had not looked after my little sister. Actually, though, she was coping better than me. Between her and Rob, they had to calm me down, or rather *hold* me down, when the nurses tried to get a cannula in the back of my hand to administer the medication. I struggled not to run screaming from the ward when the drugs quickly leaked into my hand tissue rather than just my vein so it puffed up painfully and they had to move the cannula to the other hand. I was *not* a happy camper. There were tears. And I was definitely not leading by example. I was an hysterical embarrassment of fear and distress on top of feeling, quite frankly, pants. Luckily, Rob wasn't feeling too dreadful so he could keep an eye on everyone.

'I've made a right mess of this, Rob,' I blubbered quietly through snotty, self-pitying tears once the nurse had finished hooking me up to the bag of fluids and medicines for the second time. 'Look at us, the whole group in hospital, for God's sake. All of us! What a bloody disaster.'

'Hey, it's absolutely not your fault,' he said, gently holding my puffy hand. Then added in a low voice so the others didn't hear, 'You can't take the blame for someone not taking our advice about eating ice cream. It's their damned fault, not ours. Idiots.'

'Yes, but I should have acted quicker,' I whispered back. 'Or— oh I don't know, I just can't imagine any other leader has managed to get their whole group hospitalized before. And look at the state of me. Some leader I am.'

'Bollocks,' he said. 'It's just bad luck and you feel like shit. You're doing great. They're all getting treatment. We'll all be fine once the drugs kick in.'

It's funny how your body keeps going and somehow copes until— ah, we're back to 'until' — until it just doesn't. My head hit the pillow and I had no choice but to let the antibiotics and antimalarials do their stuff as I collapsed into a morphine-induced sleep.

Things weren't the same when we got back on the road. Everyone was feeling so much better and I was thankfully back on form and feeling positive again, but from the cab, Rob and I remarked on the lack of chatter in the back. Where there had been constant spontaneous laughter previously, there was a general moroseness. It seemed that instead of being one happy family, they'd become lots of little groups. Interaction between the groups was minimal and often catty.

'They'll come round,' I said to Rob. 'They just need to readjust after hospital. They're physically better now, so it'll be okay once we get back in the swing of the trip. Anyway, the crab sorcerer will sort them out.'

'You're making it up,' he said, laughing. 'Oh, okay, go on then. Who's the crab sorcerer?'

The crab sorcerer is, as far as I know, a phenomenon unique to Cameroon. You might have heard of a crab sorcerer before if you play *Dungeons & Dragons*, but this man is a real live human being — albeit with reputedly magical abilities — living in the tiny village of Rhumsiki in the remote far north of Cameroon. He is a member of the Kapsiki tribe who live in small round stone huts with conical thatched roofs set in a landscape of majestic beauty in the Mandara Mountains. This is an uncannily otherworldly feeling place where plugs of volcanic rock once forced their way through the earth's crust to remain ever after as unashamed phallic towers, some over a kilometre high. The villagers lead simple lives growing millet and maize, keeping chickens, goats and other livestock, and, since their ancestors evaded both slavery and conversion to Islam centuries ago by hiding in these inhospitable mountains, they still mostly retain their traditions and animist beliefs.

This Cameroonian wizard is a bit of a conundrum. Not to his own people, I'm sure, but certainly to any visitors who delve a little deeper than just his 'magic'. On the one hand, he is one of the blacksmith caste of the Kapsiki tribe. Blacksmiths are deemed to be dirty and are shunned by the 'polite' society of non-blacksmith castes. This is despite them being an important part of village life due to their critical work as metalworkers plus their traditional role as the musicians of the tribe. On the other hand, the crab sorcerer is someone whom his community consult as a knowledgeable healer and gifted fortune-teller. In some respects, he has a role similar to that of a *sangoma* or witch doctor in southern Africa but he's given far less respect even though I doubt many sangomas are also skilled blacksmiths.

My old Turkish friend, Rumi, said: *You think because you understand "one" you understand "two", because one and one make two. But you must also understand "and".* I wondered how any man could live his life knowing he was considered to be a second-class citizen in his village. How could anyone accept such an injustice without the hurt and shame translating into anger or depression? Perhaps the crab sorcerer-cum-blacksmith had simply found a level of acceptance which he felt comfortable with or which he wasn't prepared to question but I guessed I would have to keep looking for the "and".

We were guided around the village and then taken for an audience with the crab sorcerer by three boys named Julius Caesar, Victor Hugo and Maggie Thatcher (honestly). Either someone in that village was very well-read and aware of international politics or the boys had cottoned on that strange names brought a good reaction and more tips from visiting travellers. Wearing shabby, indigo-dyed robes and cap, this was not a powerful-looking wizard but a rather sad-looking man in his mid-forties. He was squatting on the ground with his back to his hut. In front of him, there was the bottom half of a terracotta urn filled with sandy earth, the top half of a slightly larger urn with a narrow neck, and various bits of broken pots and sticks in a pile. We all sat around him in a semi-circle, unsure what to do.

'What is your first question?' asked Maggie Thatcher.

'Okay, I'll go,' said Emma, after a few moments of us all looking at each other wanting someone else to go first. 'Will I get married?'

Maggie translated the question and, nodding his understanding, the crab sorcerer began to position bits of tile and wood in the earth in the pot while muttering incomprehensible words which most definitely could have been a magical incantation but for all we knew could also have been an appeal for someone to get rid of these annoying tourists. I like to think it was the former as I've always loved the idea of magic — oh, and I believe in faeries; you just have to once you've watched *'It's A Wonderful Life'*. When the broken tiles were aligned to his satisfaction, he brought out a small freshwater crab from another pot. He whispered to the crab before putting it in the urn and closing it in there with the pottery lid. Then he picked up a small, handmade violin and bow and began to play and sing. Neither of the sounds were exactly music to our ears but it definitely added to the already weird experience. After one song, the lid and the crab were removed, and the sorcerer inspected what marks the crab had made and which tiles and sticks had been shifted.

'You will marry very happy,' translated Maggie, with a big smile. 'And two children.'

Others took turns to ask a question and when there were no more, I decided to ask one of my own.

'Will I come back to Africa again?'

I was happier than a sensible young woman should have been when the reply came back.

'You will come to Africa many times. This is your home.'

CHAPTER TWENTY-SIX
Roar!

Three days later, having given poor Huwey a hammering on the Cameroonian mud roads which were just the wrong side of slick thanks to a couple of days of rain, our parking brake seized on. For a whole afternoon at the side of the road, Rob and I struggled to free the jammed brakes while Sam and Emma took on the job of keeping group spirits up by baking two huge trays of flapjacks. Sam had become quite the professional at baking in our tin box of a camp oven and she always managed to sweet-talk Pete, the fire-wallah, into keeping the fire going for her at the right temperature. But Rob and I failed to fully release the brake. After spending the night by the side of the road, we drove achingly slowly into Ngaoundere the next morning and found a garage. With everyone sent off to explore the town with its huge market, Rob and I tried again, this time with the help of local mechanics. We managed to manually unwind the brakes but couldn't fix the main problem. We could at least move freely now but we were stuck without parking brakes. We ended up camping in the yard in the back of the garage that night. It reminded me of what Guy went through when we crashed in Egypt. I wondered how Guy was getting on. Would there be a letter for me in Bangui?

The last two days had been a pain in the backside, exactly what we didn't need given that the general mood in the group was still pretty negative and a good number of them seemed almost determined to be miserable.

'Look, I'm sorry about the truck problems,' I said, 'and last night's garage campsite left a lot to be desired, I know. How about we make time to go to Telo Falls for a couple of nights of swimming and relaxing in a beautiful setting before we get to Bangui? Are we all up for that?'

Sam, Maddy and Dave were immediately positive about the idea, but the rest of the group could only muster teenage-like grunts and mumblings. I looked at Rob. We were both getting more and more frustrated. Jesus, they were making it really hard to have fun.

'Great!' said Rob, ignoring the apathy. 'So now I would like to formally inaugurate a new wallaship. We need a log wallah now our brakes are buggered. Any takers?'

Dave and Alex volunteered to be at the ready with wooden blocks whenever we parked. They would ram them under our tyres to stop us from rolling anywhere. So, equipped with our new human-powered parking brake, we drove east for some time to chill out by some gorgeous waterfalls.

When we reached Bangui two days later, Rob and I worked almost non-stop for three days to fully overhaul Huwey and get everything ship-shape before we hit Zaire. Try as we might, we couldn't fix the brake problem but that wasn't going to stop our journey.

For our last night in the city, I arranged for a group meal at a restaurant that was a little like Carnivores in Nairobi, offering crocodile, warthog and antelope along with traditional African foods such as fried plantains and manioc. It was a fun evening but when we got back to camp that night, a stupid argument broke out as the bar-wallah accused the group of not writing down in the honesty book what drinks they'd taken.

'It's getting so I can't trust you lot,' he stropped. 'I'm going to lock to fridge and you've got to ask me for the key to get anything.'

The reaction was understandable disbelief from some but instant venom from others. It took Rob and I some time to calm the situation before we all headed to our tents for the night in a state of confused disquiet. I knew I was oversensitive to negativity, especially if I felt at all responsible and, let's face it, *I* was the leader, but it was just so draining and I didn't understand what was going on. I was willing to give everything in my power to make this journey a success, and I felt I was, but it obviously wasn't enough.

I collared Sam early the next morning.

'What am I missing? Why is everyone just so bloody miserable all the time now? Has anyone said anything?'

'Blimey, I've no idea. I try not to get involved. It's just weird, isn't it? Some people are even getting funny about what seats they'll sit in. We've always moved around so window seats are shared and someone's not stuck in the back, but a few won't budge now. It's not worth arguing about though, just ignore it. It'll blow over.'

After all this time, I didn't share her confidence. If we were near the end of the trip or if it had been a short trip, I would have just accepted that this group of people were sadly not meant to be travelling together. But it wasn't as easy as that. Firstly, I knew they'd all got on well for the first two months so it was hard to believe they were now so antagonistic towards each other. Secondly, we had another six weeks to go and we were about to take on four weeks in Zaire. The hardships of Zaire were tough enough with people who could pull together but I dreaded the thought of coaxing and motivating this group through the mud holes and madness I knew we faced. It could be a month of hell. What fun was that for anyone?

I took my mind off things by thinking of Guy. I'd had a lovely letter from him in Bangui and he was desperate to see me but it wasn't looking hopeful for us seeing each other any time soon.

May 1991

Hi Amanda

If you get this letter it will be a minor miracle· Yet again you don't have enough post dates· My writing is even worse than usual because it's bloody freezing here in Turkey and my hands are just too cold·

Well, surprise, surprise, I didn't get my Iranian visa again, so I had to fly over· Pakistan was quite good· I had time to head up the Karakoram Highway to Gilgit which is just brilliant·

But never mind all this travel nonsense, I'm a great deal of emotional stress at the moment· I'm missing you rotten· A couple of days ago, I asked the office what I'm doing next· The news is they've offered me South America· I'd go out at the beginning of September· I'd have to stay for a year and take over as leader after one circuit· Well, what do I do now? So far as Drago and travel is concerned, it's exactly what I wanted to do· As far as seeing you for any length of time it would

*completely fuck things up· Help! What do I do? Why
can't I see you now and talk to you about it?
You are much more important to me than South
America· But are the two mutually exclusive? How can I
know? And then there's my folks· They're getting old and
I feel bad to be considering going off for another year·*

*I've just got the letter you sent me from Nigeria· The
stuff about the hospital was extremely distressing to say
the least· I was very worried about you for a few
minutes· No, that doesn't seem long, does it, but it was
long enough for me to immediately phone Sykes to see if
you were okay· He said you were fine now, so my panic
is over, though I dare say you're feeling buggered and no
richer for such an experience· It must have been terrible·
I'm so sorry I couldn't have been there to comfort you·
In case it's not getting through or you just want to hear
me say it again: I love you!
Guy xxx*

Just before getting Guy's letter in Bangui, I'd called Crofty. He
told me that instead of flying home once I reached Zimbabwe, I
was probably going to be asked to lead a couple of short trips
from Harare to Botswana. It would be brilliant to see Botswana
but if I did that Guy would have headed off to South America for
about ten months by the time I reached the UK. If I didn't go to
Botswana I would get about a month with him. Was he worth it?
Was he as special as I thought he was? I wasn't sure how much
longer we could keep this up. Surely you had to at least spend
some time together if a relationship was to stand any chance? It

was coming up to a year since I'd seen him.

What did I really want to do? I had thought I was up for at least another year on the road but this trip was making me rethink. I absolutely loved the adventure, I was constantly captivated by the incredible places I was seeing, I thrived on the challenge and even relished the hard work, but there was no doubt that I was finding the group dynamics difficult. It was no longer about a lack of confidence, it was more that I was getting fed up with people's negativity when I couldn't see a good reason for it. For the first time since joining the company, I was beginning to consider life after Dragoman. I hadn't a clue what I wanted to do next but overlanding had opened my eyes to a bigger world, a world of opportunities that I hadn't even had the imagination to dream of before this. There were other ways to travel, other jobs to become passionate about, other lions to chase after. I just had to harness my courage and choose my lion.

'You've been very quiet this morning,' said Rob, coming up behind me as I sat by the river. 'You all right?'

I smiled at him. I was very fond of Rob. He was just such a lovely guy and I was very happy in his company. I would miss him.

We were at Kembe Falls — two days out of Bangui and two days before Zaire.

'Yes, sorry, I'm fine. I've just been doing a lot of thinking.'

'Oh God, you don't want to do that. It could hurt.'

'I think it does,' I said, 'but I've decided I can cope with the pain.'

'Ah, I see. This sounds serious. Okay, tell me. I'm listening.' He sat down on the grass next to me.

I took a deep breath.

'I've come to the conclusion that I might not be able to take this group through Zaire.'

'You're joking. What do you mean?'

'I mean . . . I mean that I know how difficult Zaire is, and although you've not been through, you know all the stories. You know it's going to be tough.'

'Yeah.'

'Well, everyone's got to pull together and work together or it'll be pure hell. I'm concerned that someone might get hurt if they're not looking out for each other. I honestly think there's a safety issue here and that's apart from the fact that everyone's supposed to be having fun and they're just not. You and I have tried to get them back on track. We've tried really hard, haven't we?'

'Yes.'

'But it's not worked. So, I'm going to talk to them all tonight after dinner and just lay it on the line about what I think about how they're acting and see if it makes any difference. It probably won't, in which case I'm going to recommend that Drago send out another leader, maybe Crofty. I think maybe a different leadership style stands a chance of bringing the group back together again. Still with you as co-driver, of course.'

'Jesus, Amanda. Are you sure? That's a big decision. And it might not work.'

'I just feel I have no option. I'm sorry, Rob. I hope you'll forgive me for ballsing up this trip for you. If what I say tonight doesn't work, it'll mean going back to Bangui and waiting for Crofty or whoever.'

'Bloody hell.'

We both sat and watched the river. The thunder of the falls added a constant white noise to the background of birdsong and clattering from the lunchtime cook team.

'Do you know what you're going to say?' Rob said, after a while.

'Roughly. I think I'm going to growl and roar at them. They'll probably hate me for it but I've decided I can cope with that . . . as long as you're okay with me doing this.'

Robbo gave me a big hug. 'I'm right beside you. But please, find the right words. I don't want you to go.'

I was super nervous and very sad but also strangely resigned to what I was pretty sure was going to be my fate after that evening: a flight home and the end of my overlanding journey. I convened a group meeting immediately after dinner was over. We were all sitting around a crackling campfire in the near darkness. A chorus of frogs and the incessant song of the cicadas were layered over the background noise of the falls. No doubt everyone thought I was going to give them an update on the next few days. I guess I was in a way.

'Well, it's going to be hard for me to say what I'm about to say, and it's possible that I'm going to upset some or maybe all of you. I apologise for that but I don't know what else to do.'

I stopped, swallowed, and looked over at Rob. He gave me a small nod and a smile. Here goes, in for a penny . . .

'You are all wonderful people. Rob and I have really enjoyed being with you so far and we've had some great times, haven't we?'

There were a few small acknowledgments but mostly a confused silence reigned. I carried on.

'You've all spent a lot of money and no doubt made sacrifices to be on this journey but I think you'd all agree that for the past three or four weeks we've not been having much fun. Since we all got ill, the mood has changed in the group. The general bitchiness going on is quite staggering. You've splintered into lots of small cliques, no-one has got any patience with anyone, and no-one is helping anyone else. We are no longer a group of friends on an exciting adventure, we are a miserable bunch of individuals on a long and difficult coach trip. We're taking our very own black cloud with us wherever we go, despite whatever wonderful things we're seeing or doing.

'So I'm wondering . . . what's the point? Aren't you? I mean, why did you all come on this journey? Is this really what you wanted? I don't believe for a minute it is. I refuse to believe that you've come all this way and spent all this money for the kind of experience you're currently having. We all have an amazing chance here to have the adventure of a lifetime. What a privilege! How many people get such an awe-inspiring opportunity as this? You are so lucky. But— but you're ruining it for yourselves. I don't know about you but I'm not enjoying this.'

I bit my bottom lip to stop myself from getting emotional and took a couple of deep breaths.

'I will hold my hands up and say that, as your tour leader, I take some responsibility for this. I've tried but I seem to have failed to cheer you all up and get us back on course. I'm sorry. I guess I could just accept that you're all adults and if you want to act this way, there's nothing I can do about it and I should just carry on. But it's not that easy. We're about to head into Zaire in a few days. I know you've all heard stories about going through Zaire — I've told you a few myself. It's hard, very hard, and to do it safely we need to be a proper team, pulling together and watching each other's backs. As your tour leader, I'm responsible for you but, to be very honest, I no longer feel I can be the person to take you through Zaire as things stand right now. Very sadly, I think that if nothing is going to change — and I mean from this very moment on, which I can see is a big ask — I'm driving us back to Bangui to contact Drago HQ and tell them they need to swap me for a different leader. Perhaps someone else can pull you all together to get you safely through the rest of the trip, still backed by the wonderful Rob, of course.'

Silence. Not even fidgeting feet. I couldn't think of anything much else to say so I decided to add one last thing then stop talking.

'Obviously, I'm gutted. I suppose I could have just arranged all this without mentioning it to you, but I guess I had one last hope that perhaps, if I was brutally honest about what I felt and how I see things, you guys might also realise what's going on and maybe you could change it. Of course, the opposite might happen and I could have just made everything worse and forced my own departure. I accept that. I feel I had no choice. You do, though. It's in your hands now. That's all I can say. Thanks for listening. I'm sorry.'

I put my head down, not wanting to look at anyone. We all sat there not looking at each other for about two minutes. It was a very long two minutes. I was just about to get up and leave when Jen spoke.

'I think Amanda's right.'

I am? Right how? Right in that I should leave? I waited.

'I think we've all been pretty dreadful to each other and I'm not enjoying it either.'

'Me too,' said Cath.

A general muttering of assent began to rise like a Mexican wave around the campfire. I wanted to cry. Had I got away with it? Had my words really touched a chord?

'For my part I'm sorry if I've been a cow. It changes tonight, I promise. I want Amanda to stay,' said Kathy.

Then Alex got up and headed for the fridge.

'Right, I hope we all agree, a fresh start. Amanda's going nowhere. She's got to show us around Zaire! Who needs a beer? And someone's got to do all that bloody washing up and plate flapping. Come on, let's get started together.'

I couldn't quite believe what I was hearing. I looked over at Robbo and he was grinning at me. He gave me a wink, went to the cab to put on some music, then started to pitch in with the clearing up. Tears only escaped when Sam came over. She hugged me tightly.

'Well done, sis. That was brave. I'm proud of you.'

'Brave? I think it was probably stupid and risky. I could have ended up going home.'

'But you didn't. You've changed things. Look.'

She was right. I had changed things. I still look back on that night in a remote spot in central Africa and can't quite believe it happened. But it did. I somehow found the right words, the ones to unlock hearts that had been temporarily barred and bolted through illness and stress. I watched as the evening completely transformed from yet another depressing night of everyone grumpily putting up with each other, to a camp that buzzed with chatter, music and joking. It was almost comical to see the effort people made to be nice to each other. There is no doubt that I was relieved but I was also very happy. I'd made a difference. Me. I'd done that.

CHAPTER TWENTY-SEVEN
In my bones

After four weeks, two ferries, umpteen log bridges and more bog holes than you could shake a smelly welly at, we said goodbye to Zaire. It hadn't been as wet as my last trip, but it wasn't a walk in the rainforest either. For me, the highlight of the journey this time had been the group themselves. True to their word at Kembe Falls, everyone pulled out all the stops to be as nice as pie to each other. It was like being back at the start of the trip when everyone had been so positive and so ready to enjoy everything.

We shared happy moments, and as we built real bridges, our bridges of friendship grew stronger. When Zairean roads threw mud at us, we made brownies. We waved together at every child we passed along the route — some tiny tots with dirty faces and snotty noses, some schoolchildren wearing smart uniforms and incongruously white shirts. We sat at roadside stalls and feasted on juicy pineapples, small sweet bananas and huge, creamy avocados. We sang songs as we drove through mile after mile of rainforest. Sometimes unable to find clearings to pitch our tents, we had cocktail parties as we camped on the mud roads.

We shared sad moments too. We looked on as men in ragged trousers walked past us with what we thought at first was a shoulder bag but then realised was dinner — a dead monkey with its tail split and looped over its head. We stared with sinking hearts as colossal overladen trucks stole away huge ancient hardwood trees from their forest home.

It was a joy and a privilege to share this extraordinary country with them.

The only serious worry during our time in Zaire was Sam. Probably due to her eczema-prone skin, she developed very bad tropical ulcers all over her legs. We kept her out of the mud holes but the ulcers carried on getting worse and she found walking so painful that eventually someone made her some crutches. I'd seen people with horrendous tropical ulcers and knew them to be no minor problem, so the stress of watching Sam in pain and danger was no fun. Thank God for Maddy who kept a close eye on her, prescribed antibiotics and kept her wounds dressed.

Africa had certainly got under Sam's skin, but for me it had gone deeper. Over the past year, it had buried itself in the very bones of me. I'd realised within a few days of my arrival that I was meant to be here and each week that passed strengthened that awareness. There was a part of me, perhaps a very old part, that belonged here. When I was twenty-three, an Indian friend once offered to read my palms. He took one look at the spider's web of deep lines on my hands and feet and told me that I had the kind of palms and soles he'd rarely seen on a European.

'You have an old soul,' he said, looking at me quizzically. 'You're more Indian . . . or maybe African.'

It was true that if you looked at my hands before my face, you'd have guessed me to be eighty. I used to want beautifully smooth hands with slim, elegant fingers but I guess they wouldn't have been quite so forgiving in the line of work I'd chosen. I had practical hands and dependably leather-like feet — with a bit more hair I'd have made a decent hobbit. Anyway, if wrinkly hands and feet made me more African, I could accept that with a smile. *Nimepokolewa maisha*. It's a Swahili phrase meaning 'I accept what life has given me.'

Right now, life had gifted me Africa. Through the heat and the dust, the tropical storms and the mud, on roads or rivers, in trucks, rafts, pirogues or on foot, I embraced whatever this bounteous continent shared with me. I was definitely the richer for it. Africa is impossible to encapsulate as one entity but when you touch its land from north to south and east to west, it engraves its name on your heart — sometimes gently, occasionally savagely. Africa! You are marked. You will always return, even if it's only in your memory.

I was certainly a marked woman. All my senses had been etched by this soul-stirring continent. The sound of drums beat a rhythm in my heart. The touch of red earth and golden sands had stained and scuffed my pale English skin. The taste of resilience and joy I recognised in the people I met along the way had melted on my tongue to be spoken of in future times. The smell of the wild — wildlands and wildlife — filled my head with the breath of freedom. The sight of sky-scraping mountains, untamed rainforests, empty deserts and wild rivers framed my fresh perspective on the world. Alongside all this, a sixth sense flowed through my veins: the spirit of Africa, the innate knowledge that this continent would remain with me forever.

Of course, nothing in life is all smiles and no tears. I'd also gained an understanding, albeit superficial, of some of the sad issues facing Africa. I'd seen the African people and the tropical rainforests being sold down the river by corrupt and greedy leaders. I'd discovered the price of an elephant's tusks, a rhino's horn, a pangolin's scales and a lion's bones — wildlife which should be protected as natural riches for us all not slaughtered for the short-term wealth of a few and supposed health benefit of the misguided. I'd learned about tribal or religious tensions and conflicts leading to the horrors of war and genocide, and natural disasters and poverty leading to displacement and malnutrition.

Light and dark. Yin and Yang. It was the way of the universe, not just Africa. It was also true of the human condition. Overlanding, especially through Africa, had taught me this. I now knew the name of the game we were playing: Life. And how magical, how terrible and how extraordinary it was.

We were due to reach Nairobi in two weeks. After a week there, we had a five-week trip down to Harare in Zimbabwe. I knew Crofty would be expecting a decision from me in Kenya. Should I stay in Africa and lead those short trips around Botswana? Or should I fly home to see Guy before he headed off to South America? Could I really abandon the chance to explore the Okavango Delta to fly five thousand miles north to see a man I'd not set eyes on for a year?

I knew the answer in my bones but it was my heart that was in charge of this decision. As always, Rumi had words of wisdom for me on this: *Your heart knows the way. Run in that direction.*

'Crofty,' I said when I called, 'I'm sorry but I've decided I'd like to fly home when I get to Harare.'

CHAPTER TWENTY-EIGHT

Your heart knows the way

A voice pierced the noisy hubbub at Heathrow.

'Taxi, Miss?'

Crofty had warned me Guy had changed. He'd lost a lot of weight, he was using a walking stick and he had— Jesus, what *was* that? Was it real? He had a small handlebar moustache. A ginger one!

It didn't matter. In fact, I didn't even really take in those details until a few minutes later. He was here, in the same space as me, breathing the same air, hugging me tightly for the longest time. It was a whole year since we'd last seen each other. Twelve months, two faxes, three phone calls, one bunch of roses, and twenty-odd handwritten letters. The months and the miles melted away.

'Come on, I'll take you home.'

Guy had an old maroon London taxi. It had no front passenger seat, so I sat in the back and we chatted through the glass window between us. I found out that the walking stick was due to a recently compacted heel.

'I accidentally got very drunk at the Dogger the other day and fell down the stairs. It bloody hurt.'

I laughed. 'Sorry. I probably wasn't meant to laugh. And what about that ginger animal on your upper lip?'

'Ah, don't you like it? I'm quite attached to it, though I was a bit surprised when it grew to be ginger rather than black.'

We chatted for a while but it was hard talking over the engine noise and my lack of sleep on the plane soon caught up with me. I lay down on the seat and fell asleep.

I expected to see narrow Suffolk lanes when I woke but instead we were on a motorway.

'Where are we?' I asked.

'Oh hello, sleepyhead. Well, I think we're just coming up to Nottingham.'

'Nottingham! Why are we going to Nottingham?'

'We're not. I'm taking you home, remember? I thought you'd want to see your folks.'

'You mean home to Durham? I thought you meant the Dogger. Blimey, I wasn't expecting that. Thank you.'

'Go back to sleep, we've still got a way to go. I'll wake you up when we get closer so you can direct me.'

When we eventually reached Mum and Dad's, no-one was home, so we went to my Nana's house just down the road. I mischievously introduced Guy as the taxi driver who had driven me from London and Nana took me at my word.

'That was very nice of him to bring you all this way,' she said, putting on the posh 'telephone' voice she reserved for people she didn't know instead of speaking in her usual broad Yorkshire. 'Thank you for bringing her home, young man.'

'Aren't you going to tell her I'm not a taxi driver?' whispered Guy.

'No,' I said. 'I'll tell her another time. Nana likes a laugh. She might be shocked when she finds you've stayed at home with us but she'll have a giggle afterwards.'

We spent a lovely couple of days at home with Mum and Dad,

then Guy suggested we head up to Scotland to see an old friend of his who he went to agricultural college with. After all the travelling we'd done, the four hours on good tarmac to Perth seemed like a quick jaunt up the road. Turning into a long driveway in the middle of nowhere, I expected we were heading for a farm worker's cottage. My jaw hit the taxi floor when there, at the end, stood the most picture-perfect white Scottish castle complete with rounded 'Rapunzel' turrets.

'Christ! This friend, he doesn't actually live here, does he?'

'Yes, Johnny's the laird of the place. Tough, eh? Like it?' He grinned.

'Well, you kept that quiet. I presume he knows we're coming?' In the garden there was a huge white marquee and a lot of activity.

'Well, actually, no. It looks like something's going on, doesn't it?'

We parked our knackered old taxi next to a top-of-the-range Range Rover. A man flanked by two boisterous black Labradors came striding around the corner. He really should have been in a kilt.

'Guy! Good God! What are you doing here? How brilliant to see you. And who's this?'

We shook hands as I introduced myself to Johnny, a whirlwind of a modern laird.

'Well, you're very welcome, Amanda. Come in, come in both of you. You've come just in time for the Grouse Ball tonight. I hope you'll stay and join us? It's sold out but I'm sure we can squeeze you in.'

I had never been in a Scottish castle before, at least not one that was still a home rather than a museum. Despite its size and the wooden panelling, high ceilings and vast windows, it was a very homely place. Johnny and his partner, Caroline, were frantic with organising everything for the ball and I'm sure the last thing they needed was two scruffy overlanders landing themselves on them without any warning but they were utterly charming and warmly welcoming. Having been given a beautiful room in one of the turrets accessed by a stone spiral staircase, Caroline took me off to find a dress to wear for the evening's event. It was black tie. I didn't exactly come prepared for a ball. We laughed as I tried on one of her beautiful dresses. We were definitely not a similar size. I'd dropped to a skinny seven stone and Caroline had a good few inches of height on me — most people do. A complimentary purple sash drew in the folds of blue taffeta around my waist and the hem slightly trailed the floor. Thank heavens it was not a full-length dress on the willowy Caroline. It was more of an off-the-shoulder than scoop-necked design on me but I looked presentable enough other than my lack of shoes. I'd only brought grubby walking boots and the tatty old leather sandals I'd worn for months now. I would go barefoot to the ball.

When I got back to our room, Guy was looking incredible in full kilted regalia. I'd never seen him in anything very smart and as for a kilt, well, I'd take that!

'I had to call the laird whose tartan this is,' he said. 'It's a family tartan but Johnny's brother is the laird of this clan tartan. I had to ask for permission to wear it.'

It was a different world. That evening there was a wealth of, well, everything. So many people looking stunning in such fine gowns and kilts, so much chatter and raucous laughter, such loud music, such an abundance of delicious food, such champagne generosity, and all within the gardens of a fairytale castle. I was in the middle of a dream, I had to be.

At the stroke of midnight, I was sure the magic would

disappear and I would find myself back in the old Dogger. But the fairy dust was strong stuff and the dream persisted.

'Are you okay? We can leave if you want. It wouldn't be rude,' said Guy, who could probably see me flagging.

'I wouldn't mind calling it a night if you're all right with that? It's been wonderful but in some ways it's hard after so long on the road and—'

'Don't worry, I know. I'm feeling the same.'

Up in our turret, the ancient stones of this sixteenth-century castle were more than up to the job of fending off the noise from the party. We were cocooned in history and crisp white linen sheets.

'Do you remember me writing to you about going to see a jeweller called Mr Lal in Jaipur,' said Guy. 'I said I'd been rather extravagant.'

'Yes.'

'Well, I forgot to show you what I bought. He made this ruby stud I'm wearing.' He pointed to his left ear.

'I noticed it. It's lovely. He's made it so well.'

'I'm glad you think so because, um . . . because I also bought this.' He reached to a bedside table and brought out a small box. Inside was a beautiful ring. It was rose gold with a tear-shaped ruby on its side and three diamonds in a row beside it.

'Amanda, I love you. Will you be my wife?'

I think I laughed. To be very honest, though, I'm not really sure what I did. It was as if my mind disappeared onto some alternate plane and my thoughts were falling over each other to be heard.

Don't be daft, woman, of course he didn't just ask you to marry him. Did he? You were never going to get married, remember? Bloody hell, that's serious. How can you be sure? Why didn't you see that coming? Marriage; that's forever.

'Amanda? Will you? Will you marry me?'

His voice cut through the chaos in my head and, suddenly, everything cleared and it just seemed so right. This was Guy — it had been right since the day we sat in the coffee shop in Cairo's Khan el Khalili.

'Yes,' I said. 'Yes, of course I will.'

Rumi was right. My heart did know the way.

I ran in that direction.

Heading back home to Durham, it felt like this journey was coming to an end. It had started back in August 1988 when I arrived at Camp Green as an imposter trainee with no spatial awareness, bad mechanics skills and very little self-confidence or courage. It was ending three years later in Durham. At one time, this was the only place I really felt I belonged, but now I also belonged in Suffolk and, of course, I'd been told by the crab sorcerer that Africa was my home too. I instinctively knew that to be true.

But that wasn't all. After travelling the equivalent of twice around the Earth — 55,000 miles by road — I realised that the whole planet was my home and that everyone in it was my neighbour, even the ones I didn't like. I had a place in this world and it was up to me to make the best of whatever life threw at me. I didn't have to put up with being mugged without a fight. I could deal with car crashes, both literal and metaphorical. I could take reasonable risks for a chance of unexpected gains or moments of joy. I could raft with river gods. I knew that most people were good people who you could trust to support you in times of need. I could learn to do most things I put my mind to — not all of them brilliantly but perhaps adequately. I knew that most broken things could be mended and if it was done properly, the fracture lines would hold up strongly and proudly. I would sometimes find the right words. I could make a difference. Yes, I would often get things wrong, but that was okay too because I'd started to learn about acceptance.

This was the beginning of a new and exciting journey but this time I wasn't chasing lions. This time I was going to learn how to love — more, better, sillily, quietly, loudly, with tears, with laughter, with pain, with hope, with joy . . . with Guy.

'She's marrying the taxi driver?' said Nana, incredulously, when Mum told her the news. 'But she's nobbut met him a minute since.'

We cleared up the confusion I'd started a few days earlier and I got a slap and a husky laugh for stringing her along. In some ways, though, she was right. Guy and I had only spent about twelve weeks in each other's company. We didn't care. We knew we fitted. Guy was due to head off to South America in just a week. He wouldn't be back until late June but that was okay, we could deal with that. We'd done it before, we could do it again, but this time I'd definitely make sure I would have at least one trip out to see him. Since I'd made up my mind I wasn't going back on the road, it would be much easier to keep in touch. Dragoman thought they might have an office job for me soon but in the meantime I would take some time out and get myself properly healthy again.

The night before we headed back down to Suffolk, there was a mellow stillness in the Durham hills. The biscuity smell of the wheat field behind the house drifted on a warm breeze into our bedroom. Guy was asleep. Perhaps I was too? All I know is that for a moment I was back in the savannah lands of Africa and I could hear a lion calling in the distance.

Thank you very much for reading *Chasing Lions*.
If you enjoyed it and feel you can help get the word out about the
book, recommendations to friends and **an online review would be
invaluable and much appreciated**.

Life after overlanding

When George told me that overlanding would 'fuck up your life', I had no idea what he meant. After about a year, it began to dawn on me. Life could never be the same again after the experiences many of us had on the road.

Overland leaders are jacks of many trades. Our days are endlessly varied and challenging, frequently fascinating and often soul-stirring. Accustomed to being our own boss for months on end, we become fiercely independent. We take responsibility for all we do and make decisions on the hoof. We find a way to deal with any situation we're faced with even if the method is not exactly textbook. We are often bodgers out of necessity, and importantly, we always try to find the fun and the positives in life.

Given all this, it's perhaps not surprising that it can be tough to return to 'normal' life. Many overlanders end up doing their own thing and becoming self-employed entrepreneurs in a variety of industries. Some decide they cannot return home and instead make their lives in Africa or other continents where they now feel more at home. A surprising number find their place within non-governmental organisations, often in the field of logistics. Many of my colleagues did admirable work for charities such as Médecins Sans Frontières, Oxfam, Save the Children or Care International, and others found themselves working with government bodies such as the Department for International Development.

After thirty years, I am still in touch with quite a lot of the leaders I worked with either on the road or in the workshop. I'm proud to call them friends. We are connected by an unusual shared experience, one which only a very small number of people have ever lived through. It gave us a certain way of looking at the world, a love for campfires, maps and seemingly unnavigable roads, a tendency to dry dishes by flapping them, and a hatred of soggy pasta served with tasteless vegetable mush.

In case you're wondering what happened to some of the people in this memoir . . .

- George, Charlie and Mike continued to build Dragoman into a world-renowned overland adventure company taking thousands of people on expeditions all over the world from Africa to Latin America and China. At a fortieth anniversary celebration in 2021, the outpouring of affection and appreciation by leaders past and present was hugely moving. We all agreed that being a Dragoman leader was the best job we'd ever had and that was in no small measure down to the three directors.
Sadly, Mike died in 2019. He is greatly missed.

- After a few years, I lost touch with Freddie (not his real name). I tried to find him through every means possible but no luck. 'Freddie', if you're reading this, please do get in touch.

- Rob went back to Australia and married another Dragoman leader. He is a proud father and keen cricketer.

- Crofty worked for many years with Save the Children Fund in the Middle East and in Africa, including in eastern DRC at the time of the first Congo war. He then headed back home to Australia to start a family and build a wholesale distribution business. He retains his relentless positivity, sense of humour and love of nicknames.

- Lutey went back to his beloved Cornwall. He initially taught technology and environmental conservation to school and higher education students through diverse practical projects. He now tinkers with an ancient woodland cottage and old vehicles. His wife and kids are ever tolerant of inflated overlanding anecdotes. He still sometimes leads expeditions, though nowadays these take the form of driving local pensioners to the supermarket in the community minibus.

- My sister Sam's African adventure did the trick and increased her confidence. After a serious car accident nearly paralysed her and put paid to her career as a chiropodist, she and her adored husband moved to Mallorca where they live happily with their adopted dog.

- Jeremy 'Joe' is a respected litigation lawyer whose hard-nosed reputation is bound to be in tatters once people know he likes messing about in mud in wellies and playing with fire. He has shared his love of travel and abiding fascination with Africa with his family.

- When I asked Stevie 'Clean' for his update I was met with some very sad news. With his permission, I'm sharing some of Stevie's moving words.

I spent five years doing emergency relief work in Iraq with my wife Cathy, who I met on one of my Dragoman Trans Africa trips in 1991. We later settled in New Zealand (Cathy's home country) and started a family. We worked hard together to build two successful small businesses, and I worked for the NZ Blood Service for five years.
Cathy survived breast cancer in 2010 but it returned in 2019. Very sadly, Cathy died aged 53 in February 2020. The Covid pandemic in March 2020 brought the loss of our second family business through a forced sale in June 2020.
So at 62, I am rebuilding my life a bit (lick your wounds,

count up what's left) working part-time, being a solo parent (Alex and Ben were 14 and 16 when Cathy died), and looking forward to retiring. Ultimately I'd like to head off to continue the unfinished adventures Cathy and I had planned.

In memory of my lovely gorgeous wife Cathy. I miss you and love you very much.

And Guy and me? Well, we married as soon as he returned from South America in 1992 and settled in Suffolk. Guy became a freelance travel writer and photographer writing articles for prestigious publications such as the Financial Times, and for six years I worked in the Dragoman office on the marketing team with Charlie.

Later, we started our own travel company and a family, but that's a tale for another time.

My thanks

My good friend Sheena Brown was responsible for introducing me to the world of overlanding. I got to share some of the early days of life at Dragoman with her when she visited me at Camp Green, and I kept in touch with her until her untimely death. I miss her.

Charlie Hopkinson, George Durie and Mike Sykes, you quite simply changed my life. I will always be grateful to you for the opportunity you gave me to lead such amazing expeditions, explore the world and find my inner lion.

To the Dragoman leaders, colleagues and travellers I included in this memoir and spent time with during my overlanding experience, I'd like to thank all of you for sharing giggles and hard work with me, and for allowing me to write about you.

To the many people who don't appear in the memoir and yet who played a part in my adventure, I send my thanks and warm wishes. It was great to share the journey with you and it wouldn't have been the same without you.

Kecia Harris, little did I know when we worked and laughed together in the workshop and drove our trucks parallel on that five-week Nairobi to Harare trip, that you would become a close lifelong friend and neighbour. Thank you for being my chief memory-jogger and first pass editor. You were unflinching in your astute criticisms (I hoped for no less!), generous in your appreciation of the story and in your suggestions, and the book simply wouldn't have been as good without your input. I'm so grateful for the time and energy you gave to me. And, by the way, I still think we looked bloody gorgeous in our new minidresses in Zanzibar!

Meg Burrows, your skillful and thoughtful editing help allowed me to polish my writing. I've ended up with a manuscript that is so much the better for your suggestions and pointers, and your annotated reactions to the story as it played out were invaluable to me in understanding how a reader might respond to each chapter or scene. Thank you for your enthusiasm and for taking the time to do this for me.

Maggie Peck, Judith Norrington and Karen Coe, thank you for beta-reading for me. It was invaluable to have such constructive feedback from people whose judgement I trust. I really appreciate you giving up your time to help me.

Dad, the strength I found to become an overlander came from you and Mum. You always believed in me. I might have doubted myself but I never doubted your faith in me. Being a parent myself, I now realise how horribly hard it must have been to say goodbye to me and not hear from me for weeks on end, and then to only get old news. You never once laid your fears at my door, so I headed off without having to carry the stress of knowing how anxious I was making you both. Sorry for your anxiety and thank you for the freedom.

Sam, thanks for deciding to come with me on our journey across Africa. It was an amazing thing to share. You were so brave when often feeling so awful, and we couldn't have managed without your cakes. Thanks for doing my washing too!

Guy, we started out as friends and learned to trust and rely on each other before we fell in love. The strength of the feelings we recognised all those years ago has never dwindled and our commitment to each other has seen us through good times and bad. Our journey continues, but thank you for agreeing to let me tell the story of the start of our relationship and share some of our letters.

About the Author

Ever since starting her overlanding career, Amanda has been a professional traveller. After nine years with Dragoman, both on the road and in the UK, she and Guy began their own travel company, Tribes Travel.

When not travelling herself or enthusing others to do likewise, Amanda has an interest in homoeopathy, trees, wildlife and nature, loves longs walks with her dog in the Suffolk countryside, and of course, she loves writing.

She has always loved the escape of reading but writing stories herself came much later. This memoir, *Chasing Lions*, is her second book. She published her debut novel, *The True,* in October 2019.

You can get in touch with Amanda through her website, Facebook or Instagram.

Www.amandamarks.co.uk

Facebook@amandamarksauthor

Instagram@andnaturewrote

Amanda is a keen supporter of bookshops — especially independents — so do ask about ordering her books at your favourite bookshop. You can also find Amanda's books online as paperbacks or ebooks, and in UK libraries.

Chasing Lions is also available on Audible.

Also by Amanda Marks

THE TRUE
An enchanting time travel tale for
nature lovers

*Buy at your local bookshop
or online*

**Lives in a remote Northumbrian valley are separated by centuries
but woven together in the heart of the trees.**

Coquetdale, Northumberland.
1725. After the final tragedy of an age-old feud, Sam's mother
disappears. His guilt-ridden search brings unexpected adventure and
romance. As a fellow of the secret order of 'The True', Sam learns to
enhance his affinity with nature, and enigmatic links across time are
revealed to him in ancient woodlands.

2000. Isolated hill-farmer, Kate, is cautiously attracted to an
intriguing stranger brought to her door by endearing runaway, Joe.
The man is certainly odd but not disturbing, unlike her stalker.
Further down the dale, Kate's woodsman cousin, Nick, falls in love
with a mysterious young woman who arrives with spring and
disappears as summer ends.

**Middle Wood links these seemingly disparate lives separated by
centuries, but is that their only connection? Does the answer lie
with The True?**

Printed in Great Britain
by Amazon